McHugh

PUFFIN BOOKS

BOY OVERBOARD

Morris Gleitzman was born and educated in England. He went to Australia with his family in 1969 and studied for a degree. In 1974 he began work with the ABC, left to become a full-time film and television writer in 1978 and has written numerous television scripts. He has two children and lives in Melbourne, but visits England regularly. Now one of the best-selling children's authors in Australia, his first children's book was *The Other Facts of Life*, based on his award-winning screenplay. This was followed by the highly acclaimed *Two Weeks with the Queen*, and he has since written many other books for children including *Toad Rage*, *Bumface*, and *Totally Wicked!* and *Deadly!* with Paul Jennings.

Visit Morris at his web site:
www.morrisgleitzman.com

MORRIS GLEITZMAN

PUFFIN BOOKS

PUFFIN BOOKS

Published by the Penguin Group
Penguin Books Ltd, 80 Strand, London WC2R 0RL, England
Penguin Putnam Inc., 375 Hudson Street, New York, New York 10014, USA
Penguin Books Australia Ltd, 250 Camberwell Road, Camberwell, Victoria 3124, Australia
Penguin Books Canada Ltd, 10 Alcorn Avenue, Toronto, Ontario, Canada M4V 3B2
Penguin Books India (P) Ltd, 11 Community Centre, Panchsheel Park,
New Delhi – 110 017, India
Penguin Books (NZ) Ltd, Cnr Rosedale and Airborne Roads, Albany, Auckland, New Zealand
Penguin Books (South Africa) (Pty) Ltd, 24 Sturdee Avenue, Rosebank 2196, South Africa

Penguin Books Ltd, Registered Offices: 80 Strand, London WC2R 0RL, England

www.penguin.com

First published in Australia by Penguin Books Australia 2002
Published in Great Britain in Puffin Books 2002
2

Text copyright © Creative Input Pty Ltd, 2002

The moral right of the author and illustrator has been asserted

Set in Minion

Made and printed in England by Clays Ltd, St Ives plc

British Library Cataloguing in Publication Data
A CIP catalogue record for this book is available from the British Library

ISBN 0–670–91408–8

Dear Reader

This is a story. It's not about an actual family, it's a story I've made up. But I couldn't have written it without help from the people who so kindly told me about their own incredible journeys.

Because I've never been a refugee and I'm not from Afghanistan, I may have got some things wrong. If so, I ask for their forgiveness, and yours.

I wrote this story to express my sympathy for children everywhere who have to flee to survive, and my admiration for the adults who embrace them at the end of their journey.

Morris Gleitzman

For
Mohammed, Marzia, Khalil,
Razia, Ruhullah and Nazia

1

I'm Manchester United and I've got the ball and everything is good.

There's no smoke, or nerve gas, or sand-storms. I can't even hear any explosions. Which is really good. Bomb wind can really put you off your football skills.

Newcastle United lunges at me. I dodge the tackle. Aziz is a small kid but he's fast and he comes back for a second lunge.

I dazzle him with footwork. I weave one way, then the other. The ball at my feet is a blur, and not just because the heat coming off the desert is making the air wobble.

Mussa, who's also Newcastle United, tries to remove my feet from my ankles. He could, he's a year older than me. But I manage to avoid his big boots and flick the ball between his legs.

'You always do that,' he complains.

Grinning, I duck past him, steer the ball round

the mudguard of a wrecked troop carrier, and find myself in front of the goal.

Only Yusuf, who's goalkeeper and referee, to beat.

Yusuf crouches between two piles of rubble, not taking his eyes off the ball at my toes.

'Over here, Jamal,' screams Zoltan, who's Manchester United with me. 'Pass.'

Normally I would. I'm known for it. Ask any of the seven kids in my school. 'Jamal's a good dribbler,' they'll say, 'and a very brilliant passer.' If I had an unexploded shell for every goal I've set up for other people, I could go into the scrap metal business.

But this time I want to score myself. I want to give a desert warrior whoop and smack the ball with all my strength and watch it whiz past Yusuf like a Scud missile.

Just once.

'Jamal,' screams Zoltan, flapping his arms like a buzzard with belly-ache. 'Over here.'

I ignore him. I decide to shoot low and try for a curve. You have to with Yusuf. He's really good at diving saves, specially for a kid with only one leg.

I can hear Aziz and Mussa thudding towards me.

I steady myself and shoot.

Hopeless.

I've sliced it. Just like last time. And all the times before that.

The ball trickles towards Yusuf. He doesn't even pretend it's a good shot. Doesn't dive on it or anything. Just picks it up and chucks it back over my head.

'Weak,' laughs Aziz behind me.

Zoltan is looking at me as though an American air strike has hit me in the head and scrambled my brains.

'Jamal,' he says. 'I was unmarked.'

'Sorry,' I say, waiting for him and Aziz and Mussa to make unkind comments about midfield players who think they're strikers but aren't.

They don't.

Nobody says a word.

I realise they're not even looking at me. They're staring at something behind me. Their faces are frozen. Their mouths are open. They're in shock.

For a horrible moment I think it's the government. Football isn't officially banned, but the government doesn't like people playing it. I think they're embarrassed that we don't have any international stars here in Afghanistan.

I turn and look fearfully at the figure behind us.

It's not what I thought. It's not an angry man in black robes with a long beard and an even longer swishing cane. It's something even scarier. A kid in a very familiar dress and headcloth.

'Bibi,' I gasp.

'Eeek,' croaks Aziz, face slack with amazement. 'It's your sister.'

For a moment there's silence except for the wind blowing in off the open desert and the distant sound

3

of someone drilling bomb fragments out of their wall in the village.

Bibi has the ball at her feet. She starts dribbling towards us.

'I want to play,' she says.

We all back away.

'No,' Mussa begs Bibi. 'You can't.'

Bibi ignores him. 'I'm sick of being stuck indoors,' she says. 'I want to play football. Come on, you soft lumps of camel poop, tackle me.'

The others are still backing away and looking at me and I realise I have to do something. This person putting us all in danger is a member of my family.

My first thought is to yell at her. Then I remember she's only nine. Two years ago I used to get distracted and forget things too. Bibi must have forgotten that girls aren't allowed to leave the house without a parent. She must have forgotten that females have to keep their faces covered at all times out of doors. And it must have slipped her mind that girls playing football is completely, totally and absolutely against the law.

'Do something,' Aziz mutters at me.

I open my mouth to remind Bibi about all this, then close it. There's no time for talk. She's only metres away from us now, eyes glinting as she dribbles the ball with her bare feet. If a government official out for a walk in the desert sees this, he'll be slashing us with his cane before I can say, 'She's only nine.' And then the government police will

4

come round to our place and drag Mum and Dad off for not controlling their daughter.

'Tackle her,' I say to the others.

They stare at me, confused.

'Get the ball off her,' I say.

Now they understand. We all lunge at Bibi. Without slowing down she sidesteps Aziz, weaves past Mussa, and flicks the ball between my legs.

I can't believe it. She's remembered every single ball skill I've taught her.

'That's not fair,' I yell as I sprint after her. 'You promised you'd only do football in your bedroom. You promised.'

She ignores me and heads for goal. Yusuf, uncertain, crouches on the goal line, eyes on the ball.

Zoltan has caught up with her.

'Bibi,' he yells. 'Over here. Pass.'

I can't believe it. All Zoltan can think about is getting a shot at goal. Suddenly I don't want Bibi to pass to him. I want her to have a shot herself.

'Me,' screams Zoltan.

Bibi ignores him. Without steadying herself or pausing to pull up her skirt, she shoots.

It's a great shot, low and hard.

Yusuf dives, but the ball scuds past his fingers and hurtles into the rocket crater behind him.

'Yes,' I hear myself yell.

'Goal for Afghanistan,' yells Bibi.

Panting, she gives me a proud grin. I grin back. Then I remember I'm her older brother and it's my job to be stern with her when she's risking everyone's safety, including hers.

Aziz and Mussa and Zoltan are staring dumbstruck after the ball, which has disappeared over the other side of the rocket crater.

'I'm going home,' says Aziz.

'Me too,' says Mussa.

'Me too,' says Zoltan.

The three of them sprint away.

'I think they're going home to practise in their bedrooms,' says Bibi. She doesn't seem to realise I'm giving her a very stern glare. 'I'll get the ball,' she says, 'then we can play one a side with Yusuf in goal.'

Before I can stop her, she's running towards the rocket crater.

'Bibi,' I yell. 'Come back.'

'Get after her,' says Yusuf, still sprawled in the dust.

Normally I'd help Yusuf to his foot after a big dive like that, but there's no time.

I sprint after Bibi.

On the other side of the rocket crater is the open desert.

Bibi must have forgotten why we don't go there.

2

'Bibi,' I yell as I scramble up the side of the rocket crater. 'Watch out for landmines.'

I can't see her. She must be in the next gully.

'Stay still,' I yell. 'Don't move.'

Please, I beg the landmines silently. Don't let her tread on you. She's only nine. This is her first time out here. Be kind.

I slither into the gully. Bibi isn't there. Neither is the ball. They can't be blown up or I'd have heard the bang.

Incredible. Her shot must have gone even further than I thought. I bet even David Beckham couldn't boot a ball that far, not over a rocket crater and a gully. Not unless it was in a cup final.

I climb out of the gully and up onto a sand dune, peering into the wind. And see Bibi. She's down on the flat desert, running towards the ball.

'Bibi,' I scream. 'Watch where you're putting your feet.'

The flat desert goes all the way to the horizon. Luckily the ball hasn't rolled that far. Luckily it's been stopped by a tank.

Dad's always saying the desert's been ruined by all the abandoned tanks and crashed planes and exploded troop carriers lying around, but sometimes war debris has its uses.

'Thank you,' I mutter to this rusting hulk as I totter down towards Bibi. I'm shaky with relief but I still manage to put my feet exactly in her footprints. If we both do the same on the way back, I'll be able to get her home safely.

As I get close to her I hear a creak. I look up and see something unexpected.

The gun barrel of the tank is moving.

Just a fraction.

Towards Bibi.

She stops running. My heart has a missile attack. Then I grin as I realise what's going on.

'It's OK,' I pant as I catch up to Bibi. 'When the tank was abandoned, they mustn't have bothered to put on the hand-brake or whatever it is that stops tank barrels moving in the wind.'

Bibi glares at me. 'What are you doing here?' she says. 'Don't you think I'm grown-up enough to get a ball on my own?'

I sigh inside. When Bibi's feelings are hurt, she usually gets violent.

'It's not that,' I say, thinking fast. 'I'm just worried about the time. If you're not back home when Mum wakes up from her nap and Dad gets back, they won't know where you are. They'll panic.'

'No they won't,' says Bibi. 'I left a note.'

'A note?' I say weakly.

'Telling them I've gone to play football.'

My throat is suddenly dryer than the rusting hulk's fuel tank.

'Bibi,' I croak. 'It's really important we go home now and tear up that note.'

'Why?' says Bibi defiantly.

'Girls playing football is a big crime,' I say. 'Almost as big as Mum and Dad running an illegal school at home. If the government finds that note, Mum and Dad are in serious trouble.'

Bibi's face falls. 'I didn't think of that,' she says.

She turns and starts to go back.

'Make sure you tread in your own footprints,' I tell her. 'I'll grab the ball and be right behind you.'

I hurry towards my ball, which is lying against one of the tank's huge caterpillar tracks.

As I get closer I see the tank isn't rusty after all. It's covered in camouflage paint. I realise something else. That throbbing noise. The one that sounds like the wind vibrating the armour plating. It's not wind, it's the throbbing of the tank's engine.

I freeze.

My brain shrivels with fear.

This tank isn't abandoned, it's parked.

I stare up at it, desperately trying to work out if the markings are American or Russian or British

9

or Iranian. Not that it makes much difference. I can't remember who's on our side this year anyway.

When I was little and I used to play tanks with empty hand grenade cases, I'd always paint the good tanks bright colours and the bad tanks dull colours. Why can't armies do that?

The tank gives a clanking lurch and a loud snort. With a horrible screech of metal, the huge gun barrel swings slowly round till it's pointing straight at me.

My insides turn to yoghurt. I want to dig a hole and hide but I know tanks have got infra-red heat-seeking devices for tracking fugitives and right now my armpits are like ovens.

'Run,' I scream over my shoulder at Bibi.

Perhaps the tank won't shoot us. Perhaps the soldiers inside are just irritable because it's really cramped and stuffy in there and one of them's got a bit of tummy wind.

It's possible, but my legs don't think so. They're wobbling so much I can't even run.

Clang.

What was that?

Clang.

A rock bounces off the tank.

I spin round. Bibi, eyes big with fury, is hurling another one.

'You squishy lumps of camel snot,' she yells at the tank. 'Give us our ball back.'

3

'Get down,' I yell at Bibi.

I fling myself to the ground, pressing my face into the dirt. Bibi stares at me for a moment, then slowly lies down.

'Buzzard wart,' she yells at the tank. She rolls onto her side and chucks another rock at it.

'Stop,' I scream at her. 'You'll get us killed.'

I'm starting to see why the government wants to keep girls locked indoors.

Something in my voice makes her stop. We lie still. Well, fairly still. My insides are quivering like goats in a bombing raid.

Bibi pulls herself up onto her elbows. 'Why are we on the ground?' she says. 'If the tank wants to shoot us, it'll shoot us.'

She's right.

We stand up. My legs only just manage it. The gun barrel of the tank is still pointing at us.

'OK,' I whisper shakily to Bibi. 'I'll talk to the

tank. You turn slowly and go straight home. And stay in your footprints.'

Bibi's eyes flash. 'I'm not leaving the ball,' she says. 'Or you.'

'Don't worry,' I say, trembling. 'I'll get the ball.' She opens her mouth to argue, but I keep on talking. 'Yusuf's back there by himself. He needs your help.'

Bibi doesn't argue with this. That's one of the good things about her. She'll argue about anything, but she'll always help a friend.

I watch her set off slowly towards the rocket crater in her own wind-blurred footsteps.

I so much want to go with her, but I can't leave my precious ball. The ball I've kept hidden from the government for nearly two years. The ball I've patched up about a million times thanks to all the jagged metal around here. The ball I love like a sister.

I turn back to face the tank. And see that the ball isn't just resting against one of the huge caterpillar tracks, it's half squashed under it.

If that tank rolls forward, my football will explode so badly not all the bike patches and love in the world can save it.

I know what I have to do.

I remember what Mum has told me about her ancestors. Fierce brave desert warriors, tall and proud in the saddles of their mighty Arab steeds. She also told me about Dad's ancestors, honest hard-working bakers, baking bread so that those fierce warriors had something to mop up their gravy. But it's my desert warrior ancestors I need to think about now.

I try not to show the tank how scared I am. I try to pull myself up to my full height, which next to a tank isn't very high. I try to make my voice sound like a desert warrior.

'Excuse me,' I say. 'Could I have my ball back please?'

Direct but polite. I think that's how a desert warrior would have said it. But with less voice wobble and bladder twitch.

The tank doesn't reply.

'I'm sorry my sister threw rocks at you,' I say. 'Please don't take it personally. She throws rocks at everybody.'

I pause hopefully, my heart going like a troop carrier stuck in first gear.

Nothing.

'Please,' I say. 'I need that ball. Football is going to be my career. Plus it's Bibi's only chance to get out and have fun and escape a life of being kept indoors by the government like all the other girls and women around here.'

I run out of breath. As I struggle to get it back I realise that talking isn't going to be enough. It never is with tanks.

Trembling, my mouth as dry as a hot bread tin, I move step by step towards the gun barrel.

This is what a desert warrior would do, I tell myself. Desert warriors didn't run away from a bit of danger. If their ball got wedged under a tank, they'd just go and get it.

I crouch and grab the ball and try to drag it out from under the tank but the pieces of metal track are thicker than my chest.

The bulging ball won't shift.

I wrap my arms round it and strain every muscle in my body, scrabbling at the ground with my feet. It's no good. The tank is too heavy.

I slump back, weak with despair.

Who am I kidding? I didn't inherit anything from Mum's ancestors. Bibi got all the desert warrior genes. All I got were Dad's. The strength, courage and fierceness of a baker.

Pathetic.

Desperation swirls inside me and makes me do a very silly thing.

'My ancestors were bakers,' I scream at the tank. 'They had really hot ovens. Hot enough to melt a dumb tank.'

I stop, my head throbbing, wondering if I'm going to die.

From inside the tank I hear radio static. Then a radio voice I can't understand because my brain's beating too loudly in my ears.

Suddenly the tank gives a lurch.

I fling myself backwards in the dirt, waiting for the ball to explode as well as most of my body parts.

They don't.

The tank is backing away. The engine is howling

and the tracks are clanking and the tank is spinning in a screeching circle. Then it clatters off, leaving me choking in its dust.

I grab my ball and hold it to my chest. I love the smell of the leather, even though Bibi reckons it's made from camel. I even love the smell of the rubber patches.

I watch the tank roar and shudder towards the horizon.

'Thank you,' I croak.

I wave, but nobody waves back.

I stand up, dizzy with relief. I thank my ancestors. Even if the desert warriors aren't listening, I know the bakers are. Dad always says you can trust people who get up at 3am and he's right.

The tank has gone. Everything's OK. It's still a good day.

Then I hear a scream in the distance. A long terrified scream.

Bibi.

I turn and start running back towards her.

Yusuf is yelling. His voice is high-pitched with panic.

'Jamal, Jamal, come quickly. Your stupid sister's stepped on a mine.'

4

No bang.

That's all I think as I claw my way up the side of the rocket crater towards Bibi. Rubble scrapes my fingers raw, but I hardly notice.

No explosion.

That's good.

Unless . . .

Unless I missed it when the tank was screeching. Or it was muffled by Bibi's long skirt. Or someone's invented a silent landmine.

I stop thinking about that and keep climbing.

I can't smell any explosion. That's good too. When Yusuf's grandfather demonstrated a land-mine exploding to us kids in the village the smell was gross. Worse than Mussa's socks.

'Hang on, Bibi,' I shout frantically. 'It's going to be OK.'

They can't hear me. Yusuf is yelling too loudly and Bibi's screams are filling the air like desert birds after a battle.

Please, I pray. Don't let her legs be blown off. Not even just one.

I fling myself over the rim of the crater.

Bibi is on the other side of the football pitch, surrounded by war wreckage. She's standing rock still, one leg straight, the other crooked. Yusuf is kneeling next to her straight leg, pushing down with both hands on her foot.

As I run to her I see what's happened. The mine hasn't gone off because Bibi's weight is still on it. If she moves her foot off the metal plate, the mine will explode.

'Bibi,' I yell. 'Don't move.'

It's a dumb thing to say and I can see from the tearful glare Bibi gives me that she thinks so too.

I drop to my knees and press my hands on top of Yusuf's.

'Ow,' says Bibi. 'That hurts.'

'Why didn't you keep an eye on her?' I shout at Yusuf.

Immediately I wish I hadn't said that. Yusuf looks as miserable as I feel.

'I'm sorry,' I say. 'It's not your fault. The government's supposed to have cleared all the mines this close to the village.'

'That's what they said seven years ago,' mutters Yusuf, sliding one hand off Bibi's foot and rubbing his leg stump inside his baggy shorts. 'I'm sorry, Jamal.'

'It's my fault,' says Bibi. 'I saw something I wanted for my bird migration project.'

She's pointing to a chunk of rusty debris nearby. An entire wing section off a fighter plane.

I don't say anything. I can feel Bibi's foot trembling. Her lips have gone pale. The poor thing's terrified. This is not the time to remind her that our school is meant to be secret and it won't be secret much longer if she starts dragging ten-metre pieces of project material into the house.

'What are we going to do?' she whimpers.

'Don't worry,' I say. 'I'll think of something. Just remember the secret of football. Never give up, even when things are looking hopeless.'

Bibi bursts into tears again.

'Don't say hopeless, you camel poop,' she yells.

I look around for help. The village isn't that far away and I know Yusuf will hop like the wind if I ask him, but I don't. If the wrong people come to rescue Bibi and see she's a girl, she'll be in almost as much trouble as she is now.

There's only one thing to do.

I stand up and put my foot next to Bibi's.

'OK,' I say. 'Slide your foot off the metal plate while I slide my foot on.'

Bibi gawks at me. Yusuf's mouth is hanging open too.

'Are you sure?' he whispers. 'If that plate pops up, the mine'll explode.'

Yusuf's got a good heart, but he can be a bit of a

18

referee sometimes. I don't mind. He's only my age but he's taller than me and he's already got hair on his leg.

'I'll be careful,' I say, struggling to look confident. 'Come on Bibi, just slide your foot off slowly.'

'But then you'll be on the mine,' says Bibi. 'You could be blown up.'

'I won't,' I say. 'It's probably a dud mine anyway. A lot of these landmines are twenty years old and totally clapped out. Aren't they, Yusuf?'

Yusuf doesn't say anything. He's probably not the best person to be asking.

Bibi is staring at Yusuf's empty shorts leg.

'No,' she yells. 'It's too risky.' She crumples into tears again.

'Bibi,' I say desperately. 'If you get blown up, people will find out you've been playing football. Even if I tear up the note.'

Bibi shakes her head. 'Mum and Dad will understand,' she replies. 'They're always doing things they're not meant to. Like school, and Dad putting army petrol in his taxi that time.'

I'm getting frantic and I can see Yusuf is too. I'm hoping the mine's a rusted dud, but it might not be. Yusuf's grandfather says that some old mines are seriously unstable. Some go off even before the metal plate flips up.

I've got to get Bibi away from here.

'What about the government?' I say to her. 'If the government finds out a girl's been playing football, Mum and Dad are in big trouble, remember?'

Bibi thinks about this. I can see she knows it's true. But instead of getting off the mine, she gets angry.

'It's not fair,' she yells. 'I don't want to get blown up and I don't want you to get blown up either. It's not fair. '

This is bad. She's working up to a tantrum. When Bibi has a tantrum she stamps her feet.

I grab her shoulders and put my face close to hers.

'Listen,' I say. 'Let me step on the mine. Then Yusuf will help you get home, and once you're inside he'll bring help for me. We'll all be fine.'

'He's right,' says Yusuf.

Bibi glares at me for a long time. 'OK,' she says finally. 'If I die, I hope you do as well.' Then her eyes fill with tears again and she puts her arms round me. 'Because if I was dead and you weren't, I'd really miss you.'

She shuffles off the mine, Yusuf holding her feet so she doesn't move too fast.

I shuffle on at the same time.

In the tension of the moment I forget Bibi is meant to be sprinting away. We hold each other tight while we wait and see what happens.

Nothing.

I can feel the spring of the mine pushing against the soles of my feet, but the mine doesn't explode.

'OK,' I say to Yusuf. 'Run for it.'

It's not a very thoughtful thing to say to a kid with

one leg, but I know Yusuf doesn't mind. He grabs his crutches with one hand and Bibi with the other.

She's still holding on to me, her dark eyes staring at me fiercely. 'Jamal,' she says, 'I like football and I'm going to keep on playing it.' She hugs me, then thinks of something. 'Unless you're dead, because then I wouldn't feel like it.'

She gives me a final hug and hurries away with Yusuf.

I look down at the metal plate under my feet.

It doesn't look very rusty. It looks quite new. Which is good. New mines are better. The coloured wires haven't faded and the bomb disposal experts can see which ones to snip.

Of course, if I was a desert warrior, I'd have a go at snipping them myself.

No. Don't even think about it. Bomb disposal experts do years of training, plus practise at stopping their hands shaking. Best to leave it to them.

Even though my hands are shaking, inside I'm feeling more relaxed.

Then I hear Bibi yelling my name and I get tense again.

I look up.

Bibi is running towards me, sobbing.

'I can't,' she's yelling. 'I don't want to leave you.'

I watch in horror as she flings her arms round me and buries her face in my chest. I try to bend my legs to absorb the impact like David Beckham does when a defender barges into him, but Bibi is moving too fast and together we sway and totter.

And fall.

Off the mine.

We cling to each other in the dust and scream for a long time. When we realise we're still alive, we stop.

We stare at the metal plate.

It hasn't flipped up.

No bang.

We get up and I've never felt so faint or sick or dizzy.

'You pongy lump of camel spleen,' Bibi yells at the mine. 'I'd like to kick you in the guts.'

As I take her arm and drag her towards the village, I start to feel better. We've survived. We're not dead. Even though Bibi's not safely home yet, and I may throw up at any minute, life is good.

5

We creep into the village through a row of houses that are mostly rubble.

A truck goes past and we duck down, just in case. You can never be sure with trucks. Sometimes they're just smugglers, but sometimes they're the government.

A rock bounces off the back of the truck.

'Bibi,' I hiss. 'Stop it.'

'I hate trucks,' she growls. 'Trucks took Anisa's dad away and she's never seen him again.'

When the truck has gone, we help Yusuf back onto his crutches and hurry towards our house.

'I hate this whole country,' says Bibi after a while. 'This country is camel snot.'

I'm shocked.

Nine-year-old kids shouldn't hate their country. They should love their country and want it to do well in the World Cup and earn the respect of other nations so they'll stop bombing us.

I push Yusuf's hat further down over Bibi's ears and pull my jacket tighter round her shoulders and check she's still got her skirt rolled up.

'Keep your voice down,' I whisper. 'You're meant to be a boy.'

'I don't care if I'm meant to be a goat,' says Bibi. 'This place is a bum boil.'

Yusuf's shocked too. He almost falls over.

Luckily the people in the streets are too busy to notice. When your house keeps getting bombed you've always got a lot of chores.

We turn the corner into our street. I look anxiously towards our house.

Everything is good. Mum's shutters are closed which means she's still asleep. Dad's taxi isn't there. We can get inside without being caught. But only if Bibi stops complaining so loudly.

'I bet Manchester hasn't got landmines,' she says bitterly.

'It might have,' I whisper to her. 'They might just not show them on satellite TV football coverage.'

'I don't think Manchester has got landmines,' says Yusuf, frowning. 'Not unless they were put there by Liverpool supporters.'

'Anyway,' I say to Bibi. 'We should be grateful. Our house has still got a roof. Our mum and dad are still alive. We've got all our arms and legs. Compared to some people we're really lucky.'

Bibi gives me a look and glances apologetically at Yusuf.

'My house has still got a roof,' says Yusuf indignantly.

Bibi digs me with her elbow. 'Nice one,' she hisses.

'Sorry,' I say to Yusuf. 'I didn't mean you.'

'That's OK,' says Yusuf, and does an armpit raspberry. His arms are really strong, so he can do really good ones.

As we creep towards the house, I bounce the ball on Bibi's head a couple of times to make her pay attention.

'All I'm saying,' I tell her, 'is that things could be worse.'

On the third bounce, a big pair of hands grabs the ball.

'Gotcha,' bellows a furious voice.

It's Mr Nasser. He's the angriest man in our street, and the tallest, and he's got really scary nose hair.

'Run,' I say to Bibi.

I want to run too, but I can't leave Yusuf or the ball.

Mr Nasser grabs Bibi by the shoulder. She tries to wriggle free. Yusuf's hat starts to slip off her head. Any moment her hair could flop out and the edge of her skirt could drop down from under my jacket.

'You boys broke my window,' yells Mr Nasser, pointing to one of his downstairs windows. 'Look, broken.'

He's partly right. The window is broken. But it wasn't us. OK, we might not always obey the law, but we'd never play football in the street.

'It wasn't us, Mr Nasser, honest,' I say.

I can see he doesn't believe us. He's not even listening. Since his wife got ill and died, he never listens to anybody.

'Jamal's got too much skill to break a window,' says Yusuf, pushing himself in front of Mr Nasser and pointing to me.

He's trying to distract Mr Nasser from Bibi. She's trying to kick Mr Nasser and the effort is making her hair slip out from under the hat.

'Go on, Jamal,' says Yusuf. 'Show him.'

Trembling, I take the ball before Mr Nasser realises what's happening. I drop the ball onto my foot, flick it to my knee, bounce it on my head, catch it with my foot and start the whole thing over again.

Mr Nasser is staring, bemused.

Behind him, I can see Yusuf trying to calm Bibi down and stuff her hair back under the hat.

I shouldn't have looked. 'Never take your eye off the ball,' that's what Mum's ancestors would say if they were here.

The ball is dropping off my head, but it isn't going anywhere near my foot.

I lunge for it.

I make contact.

The ball flies off my foot and into Mr Nasser's other downstairs window.

The glass breaks.

'Vandals,' screams Mr Nasser. 'Criminals. I'm calling the police.'

Yusuf is staring at me in shock. Bibi is looking paler than when she was standing on the landmine.

'Sorry,' I say to them all.

'I'm reporting this,' roars Mr Nasser. 'To your parents.'

'No need,' says a voice.

I spin round.

Dad's taxi has pulled up and Dad is getting out, looking grim.

He picks up the ball, strides over to us, grabs me by the ear and turns to Mr Nasser.

'I'm sorry about this, Mr Nasser,' he says. 'As this boy's father I take full responsibility. I will of course pay for your windows. I don't think we need involve the police.'

Dad is shorter than Mr Nasser, but he's much younger. His eyes are very bright. It makes people think he's fierce, but it's actually eye strain from driving the taxi so much at night.

Mr Nasser takes a step back.

Then Dad notices Bibi. He opens his mouth to say something, but changes his mind. He glances anxiously at Mr Nasser.

'Please be so good as to leave these other, um, boys in my hands,' he says to Mr Nasser. 'I will make sure they are dealt with strictly by their parents.'

I can see Bibi looking furious. I know she wants to tell Dad we only broke one of the windows. Silently I beg her to keep quiet.

She does.

Dad puts the ball under his arm and grabs Yusuf's ear too. He drags me and Yusuf to the taxi and pushes us into the back seat, crutches and all. He puts Bibi in the front next to him.

'You will have payment and a written apology tonight, Mr Nasser,' he calls out the window.

Mr Nasser stands glaring at us. I can see he still wants to report us to the police. I hope desperately that the thought of money will calm him down.

The taxi engine has stalled, which it always does. By the time Dad has got it started again, Mr Nasser has gone into his house. Dad drives us down the street to our place.

'You,' he says to Yusuf. 'Off home. I'll be seeing your grandfather later.'

Yusuf gives me a miserable look as he gets out of the taxi. As I hand him his crutches I give him a look to let him know how grateful I am for his help saving Bibi.

Then I look at Dad.

I'm hoping Dad isn't as angry as he seems. I'm hoping he's only been pretending to be angry for Mr Nasser's sake. Sometimes, when Dad isn't really angry, he gives us a wink to let us know.

It doesn't look good.

Dad isn't winking.

6

I stand in our living room, waiting for Dad to yell at me.

I can hear him in the bedroom talking to Mum, which is a bit strange. You'd think he'd yell at me first, then tell Mum about it. Perhaps he's asking Mum to help him yell at me. She's a teacher, so she's more experienced at yelling.

Bibi punches me in the arm.

'Sorry for causing so much trouble,' she whispers.

I rub my arm and give her a grateful smile.

'That's OK,' I say. 'It was a great goal. You're a better kicker than me.'

'You might improve with practice,' she says.

I decide not to tickle her for being cheeky. 'Thanks,' I say. Perhaps she's right. Perhaps that's how bakers get to be desert warriors. Practice.

Bibi punches my arm again.

'We have to tell Mum and Dad we only smashed one window,' she hisses, eyes shining fiercely. Then she frowns. 'They probably won't believe us. Not now we've broken the law with me playing football.'

'They might like the idea,' I say, nodding towards the bedroom. 'They might be glad you've been getting some exercise.'

You've got to hope.

Bibi doesn't look even a tiny bit hopeful.

Then Mum and Dad come out of their room and I don't feel hopeful any more either. Dad's face is pale and grim. Mum's eyes are red and her lips are thin with stress.

I brace myself for yelling.

But it doesn't happen. Instead, Mum and Dad put their arms round me and Bibi. They squeeze us both tight. I can't believe it. A family hug. They must be pleased about Bibi getting the exercise. Wait till I tell them how good she is at kicking.

'Jamal and Bibi,' says Mum softly. 'You know we love you very much.'

'Yes,' I say, glowing with happiness and relief.

'Yes,' says Bibi. She sounds pretty happy and relieved too.

'No matter what happens,' says Mum, 'you two are the most precious things in our lives.'

'I know,' I say quietly. It's true. Mum and Dad's parents are all dead in the war, and Dad's brothers. There's only the four of us left.

Mum is crying. I can feel her tears on my head. I don't understand. I'm pretty sure she's not crying about the broken window. She must be thinking about our poor dead relatives. Now I'm thinking about them, my eyes start to fill up too. Not with painful tears, with the other kind. I'm just so grateful the four of us are here together, safe.

Dad crouches down and looks at me and Bibi. I've never seen his face so serious.

'We've got to leave this house,' he says.

I stare at him, stunned.

'What?' I say.

Dad bites his lip and looks like he can't believe it either. Then he clenches his teeth and carries on.

'We've got to get out of the house,' he says. 'Tonight. And we can't ever come back.'

I feel like a landmine has just exploded next to my head. My brain can hardly take in the words.

Then I realise what has happened.

'It's not that bad,' I gabble. 'Mr Nasser probably won't go to the police. And nobody saw Bibi playing football, honest. We don't have to leave.'

'The landmine didn't even go off,' says Bibi.

Mum stares at her. I can see Mum is having trouble taking everything in too. She gives a big sigh and a sob comes out with it.

'It's not that,' says Mum. 'It's not any of that.'

'Then why do we have to leave?' I say frantically. 'Is it the brake lights on the taxi?'

It's not fair. The government shouldn't persecute a person just because their brake lights are temporarily out of order.

'It's not the brake lights,' says Dad quietly. 'It's

something much more serious than that.'

I knew it. The army petrol Dad bought from that other taxi driver. Dancing donkeys, he only did it once. He was desperate. You just can't be a taxi driver without petrol. Passengers hate it when you switch the meter on and then ask them to get out and help you push the taxi.

Mum takes a deep breath and wipes her eyes and I see she's got chalk dust on her cheek.

'It's the school,' she says quietly. 'The government has found out about our school.'

Suddenly it hits me. I look around the living room. All the school stuff has gone. Normally our living room is a fully equipped school for eight kids. Blackboard. Floor mats. Books. Paint brushes that we're always squabbling over because there are only three of them.

All gone.

'How did the government find out?' I ask, my voice wobbly with shock. But I already know. School transport. The other girls in the class can't be seen walking to school so they have to be transported in secret. Someone must have seen Dad picking Anisa and Fatima up at their houses. Or dropping them back in the afternoon. It's always been a big risk, doing that every day, even though Anisa and Fatima always travel in the boot.

Mum is staring at the place on the wall where her beloved blackboard used to hang. Now I understand why she's crying.

Dad puts his arms round me and Bibi again. I can feel him trembling.

'We don't know how the government found out,' he says. 'We just know they have. Someone I trust told me an hour ago. It's too risky to stay. We have to pack up and leave right now.'

7

I'm so angry I could punch a tank.

I don't because there isn't a tank in our living room. Plus I'm in too much shock to punch anything.

Dad's in the other room, rolling up the prayer mats and packing them into a bag. Mum's taking a picture I painted in class off the wall.

This can't be happening.

We can't just be abandoning our home.

Dad only finished replacing the cracked mudbricks in my room last week. He promised if I'm good I can have lino on the floor.

I don't want to go.

Bibi doesn't either.

'If that camel dung government comes round here,' she hisses, 'they'll get a faceful of rocks.'

She kicks the living room wall. Mum grabs her and hugs her tight. Bibi's shoulders slump and her whole body starts shaking.

'Mum,' she sobs in a tiny voice. 'I'm scared.'

I know how she feels.

I can see Mum just wants to hug Bibi for several hours, but instead she goes over to the candlestick cupboard. She takes the candlestick out and unwraps the old blanket from around it. Even though the room is getting gloomy in the dusk, and the candlestick is a bit grimy with soot and wax, it glows in her hands. Specially the precious stones.

Mum turns to me and Bibi.

'This will keep us safe,' she says.

Bibi stops crying. The candlestick's been in Mum's family for hundreds of years. Her ancestors used to burn a candle before they went into battle. Mum has always told us that as long as we've got it, we'll be safe. And it's true. Mum has burned candles through some really long air raids and we've never had a scratch, except for the taxi.

I wish she'd burn a candle now so we don't have to leave.

Mum gently wipes Bibi's eyes and nose with her sleeve. That's one of the great things about Mum. She doesn't mind wiping up dribble even when it's not hers.

'Jamal,' says Mum. 'Go into your room, pull your curtain down and knot it into a bag you can wear on your back. Pack your clothes into it and whatever else will fit.'

I stare at her, praying she'll change her mind and say we can stay.

'Now,' she says.

It's the voice she uses in class when I'm day-dreaming about football or when Bibi's getting carried away in a debate. But we're not the ones getting carried away now. They are. Dad's in their room, stuffing clothes into a bag. Mum's heading into Bibi's room to get Bibi started on her packing.

I go into my room, but my arms are too heavy to lift up to the curtain. Instead I just stare sadly at the things that won't fit into a rucksack. My tanks made out of hand grenade cases. A bleached bone that Yusuf reckons is the leg bone of a fighter pilot who crashed in the desert and got eaten by scorpions. My cardboard footballs, the ones I made before Dad bought me a real one.

After a while I hear Dad come out of his room and go down to the cellar.

I follow him.

Halfway down the steps I stop.

In the flickering candlelight I can see Dad standing at his oven. The oven that was his father's and his grandfather's too.

Dad loves that oven. That's why he gets up at 3am each morning and bakes bread even though he hasn't got a baker's shop and has to sell it in the taxi.

Dad is stroking the warm bricks. I can't hear what he's whispering, but I can see the sadness in his face and I realise he's saying goodbye to his oven.

Then I see that Mum is down here too. She's got the spade and she's digging a hole in the dirt floor of the cellar. Piled up next to the hole are the school mats and books and paint brushes. And the blackboard in pieces.

Mum's burying our school.

My eyes fill with tears again to see that. This time they're painful tears. Mum and Dad look so miserable.

None of us want to leave.

I see something on the cellar floor next to the pile of school stuff. It's my painting, the one Mum took off the living room wall, the one of me scoring a goal in the World Cup final.

I go down the steps and pick it up and peer at it in the gloom. In the painting I don't look like a baker, I look like a desert warrior.

I dry my tears.

Suddenly I'm determined to do it.

Find a way for us to stay.

8

'Overboard,' chuckles Yusuf's grandfather. 'They're saying he's gone overboard.'

I stare at the TV, puzzled. I've been watching the match, but I haven't really been thinking about it. I've been trying to think of a plan so we don't have to leave our home.

On the screen, a Liverpool player is being sent off by the referee for kicking the Chelsea goalkeeper in the head. The referee is angrily showing him a red card. The crowd is booing. The commentators are talking excitedly.

It looked like an accident to me. The Liverpool striker was attempting a spectacular scissor kick and the poor Chelsea goalie's head got in the way.

'Overboard,' chortles Yusuf's grandfather, his long beard jiggling with amusement.

I wish he'd laugh a bit more quietly. Bibi's asleep. If she wakes up and finds Mum and Dad aren't here she could get panicked, even though they've just gone to warn the parents of the other kids from school. Yusuf's grandfather's cellar is a pretty scary place for a little kid. Specially the souvenir Simpsons tea towels from London stuck all over the walls. In Afghanistan, if a person's skin goes yellow it means they're probably going to die.

I glance over at Bibi. Luckily she's still asleep. And Yusuf has dozed off on the mattress next to her.

'Why are they saying the Liverpool player went overboard?' I ask Yusuf's grandfather. 'There's no boat there. It's a football pitch.'

'Ah,' chuckles Yusuf's grandfather. 'You ask hard questions.'

That's the problem with watching football on Yusuf's grandfather's illegal satellite TV. I don't speak English so I can't understand what the commentators are saying. Luckily Yusuf's grandfather does because he lived there once.

'In English,' says Yusuf's grandfather, 'the word overboard also means to do something that is bold, wild, dangerous and daring.'

I'm not sure exactly what he means.

'For example,' he says, seeing my frown. 'If a desert mouse urinates on the electrical wiring of an anti-aircraft gun, hoping to make it fire and shoot down a plane so he can see if there's any cheese in the pilot's lunchbox, that's going overboard.'

Now I understand. My heart is beating faster. I stare at the screen.

'Do you want me to take Yusuf up to his own

bed?' asks Yusuf's grandfather. 'So you can have the mattress?'

'No thanks,' I say. 'I'm not tired. I'll watch some more football if that's OK.'

I've got too much to think about to go to sleep. You don't feel like sleep when you've just decided to go overboard.

'That's fine,' says Yusuf's grandfather. 'I'll watch with you. Until your parents get back.'

The next match is Charlton Athletic fighting for survival. If they lose this game against Manchester United, they'll be relegated out of the English Premier League and their lives will be full of shame, misery and grief.

While they play their hearts out, I carry on trying to think of a plan.

I wish I could go to the city and get the government out of bed and tell them what they're doing to our family. How they've made my mum cry. How they've stopped me getting lino. But I can't. I don't even know where the government lives.

Manchester United are playing magnificently as usual, and Charlton are struggling bravely. Very bravely. They score the first goal. Their fans roar. And that's just in the stadium. I know that all around the world other Charlton fans are watching TV and cheering and weeping and hugging each other. At this moment they'd do anything for their brave Charlton warriors.

Suddenly it hits me.

A plan.

Just as suddenly the TV picture goes fuzzy. The government has banned TV, so Yusuf's grandfather has installed his illegal satellite dish on a wrecked military communications tower at the edge of the village where it won't be noticed. Trouble is, the picture goes fuzzy every time there's a sand-storm or a plane flies over or a jackal scratches itself in the desert.

Tonight I don't care because my brain is already going overboard.

'If I get very good at football,' I say to Yusuf's grandfather, 'do you think the government will forgive Mum and Dad?'

Yusuf's grandfather looks at me. I can see he's not sure what I'm on about.

'If a person gets really good at football,' I say, 'so good that he inspires the government to start a national team, so good that he helps them do really well in the World Cup, do you think the government would stop being cross with that person's parents even if that person's parents had been running an illegal school?'

Yusuf's grandfather stares at me for a long time.

'It wouldn't matter if they stayed a bit cross,' I say after a while, 'as long as they let that family live in their own village without bullying them.'

Yusuf's grandfather reaches across and grips my shoulder. He's never done that before.

'Jamal,' he says, his voice sort of thick. 'You are a

good boy. But things are very difficult for us. Our people are not liked by many of the other people in this country. This has been going on for hundreds of years.'

I nod. Mum taught us this in school. Yusuf's grandfather knows a lot for a person whose TV only picks up the sports channel.

'Our problems are many,' says Yusuf's grandfather. 'They started long before this government.'

A tear is rolling down his cheek into his beard.

I stare at him and suddenly I realise just how important my plan is. If I can become the star of the Afghanistan national football team, perhaps that'll make all of us more popular, not just me and Mum and Dad and Bibi. Perhaps none of us will ever be threatened or bullied or killed again, not by the government or anybody.

It's a good plan.

A really good plan.

But to make it work I need practice.

9

This is the perfect way to get extra football practice.

Wait till everyone in the house is asleep, then sneak outside and dribble down the middle of the street like I'm doing now.

The neighbours are all asleep too so you don't get arrested and imprisoned. Unless you make too much noise. You know, cheer your own ball tricks or describe your own footwork in a loud commentator's voice.

I'm not doing that.

Silent skill, that's me.

Off the foot, onto the knee, onto the head, back onto the foot.

It's also a really good way for a person who can't sleep to take his mind off things he's a bit worried about. Like why Mum and Dad aren't back yet. Out here he might be able to see if they're in any danger. This moonlight's almost as bright as Manchester United's stadium with the electricity switched on.

Foot, knee, head, foot.

Hello Sir Alex Ferguson, manager of Manchester United, I didn't see you there. A place in the Manchester United youth team? I'd be delighted. Thank you very much. You're right, Sir Alex, that would make the government a bit embarrassed they'd tried to persecute our family.

'Jamal, what are you doing?'

A voice, hissing at me out of the shadows.

I freeze, my legs trembling, my guts knotted. I peer into the gloom.

'You're playing football in the street,' hisses the voice.

Relief gushes through me. 'Mum?' I whisper. 'Dad?'

But it isn't either of them. It's Bibi. She comes towards me, eyes as big as stadium floodlights.

'Keep your voice down,' I whisper.

She doesn't. 'I saw you creeping out of the cellar,' she says accusingly.

I sigh. That's exactly what I hoped wouldn't happen. That's why I didn't risk opening my rucksack and making a noise getting my ball. That's why I borrowed Yusuf's.

'That's Yusuf's ball,' says Bibi, even more accusingly.

'I know,' I say, wondering how I can get her back into the cellar without waking up the neighbours.

'Where are Mum and Dad?' she demands. Her eyes have a dangerous glint that means either tears or violence.

I explain about Mum and Dad going to warn the parents of the other kids from school.

'They'll be safe,' I say. 'They're in disguise. They borrowed robes from Yusuf's grandfather.'

It's not true, but I can see it makes Bibi feel better, and in a weird way it makes me feel better too.

'I want to play,' says Bibi.

Before I can stop her, she flicks the ball away from my feet. I lunge at it, but she sidesteps my tackle and steers the ball down the street. She turns and dribbles towards me.

'Come on,' she says. 'Get it from me.'

I go in with my fastest tackle, but she flips the ball over my ankle, runs round the other side of me and traps the ball under her foot.

I stare at her, half angry, half grinning. This is amazing. My sister is a football natural.

A wonderful thought hits me. We can do it together. We can improve our skills and impress the government and start a national team and win the hearts of all Afghans together. When the government sees how talented Bibi is, they'll change their minds about girls playing football. They'll have to.

'Penalty shot,' says Bibi, eyes gleaming. She steps back, hitches up her skirt, runs at the ball and boots it.

Hard.

The ball flies up the street. For a sickening second I think it's going to smash through Mr Nasser's one unbroken window. But it curves away from his house and sails all the way up the street.

And thumps into the door of our house.

It's the most incredible kick I've seen in my life.

'Wow,' I whisper.

Then our house explodes.

A white flash lights up the whole village and half the desert. A roar of wind smashes into us and flings us both to the ground. I roll onto Bibi and try to cover as much of her body with mine as I can while the air rips at us and stones rain down on us. People are screaming and running out of houses.

'Get off,' yells Bibi. 'You're squashing my head.'

I roll over and peer down the street through the dust.

Our house is gone. Where it was is just a dark gap between the other houses. Rubble is lying where Dad used to park the taxi.

I stare, speechless, ears ringing, trying to take it all in.

My mouth is open and full of grit.

It was a hard kick, but it wasn't that hard.

Then I hear engines revving. Two trucks are speeding away down the side street.

Someone is pulling me and Bibi to our feet. It's Dad. His eyes are wide and he's breathing hard and staring at the trucks as well.

'Pigs,' he hisses.

Dad hardly ever uses bad language like that. Unlike most taxi drivers he never swears at other drivers. There's really only one thing he ever swears about. That's how I realise what's happened.

The government has blown up our house.

10

Dad carries me and Bibi down the steps into Yusuf's grandfather's cellar. A panicked thought jabs into my bruised and numb brain.

'Where's Mum?' I ask.

Either my voice is still bomb-affected or Dad pretends not to hear. He puts us down and dashes around the cellar, grabbing our rucksacks.

'Dad,' insists Bibi, her eyes wild and face streaked with dust. 'Where's Mum?'

Dad stops and takes a deep breath. He kneels next to us and puts his finger over Bibi's lips.

'It's OK,' he says softly. 'Mum wants us to go to the city. She'll meet us there tomorrow.'

We both stare at him.

The city? Tomorrow?

'Why?' says Bibi, her voice wobbly with panic. 'What's she doing?'

Dad takes another deep breath. He looks like he's trying to think what to say next.

I'm starting to feel as panicked as Bibi.

'Mum wants me to take you somewhere safe,' says Dad. 'We're going to a place in the city, and we'll see Mum there tomorrow. She'll be fine. Trust me.'

I do trust him. He's my dad. He never lies unless it's to protect people.

'If Mum's not OK,' says Bibi in a fierce wavering voice, 'I'll be really really cross.'

Dad gives us a squeeze and glances up the cellar steps.

'Yusuf,' he calls. 'What's happening outside?'

Yusuf's crutches appear at the top of the steps. Then his head.

'Everyone's still out there,' he says. 'The street's packed.'

I can hear them. People from all over the village, talking about the explosion and wondering where we are. Some people are yelling that they've found bits of us.

People in this village have got very vivid imaginations.

Yusuf's grandfather hurries down the steps. 'Taxi's not damaged,' he says. 'And nobody's found it in the alley yet.'

Dad looks relieved. Well, not relieved exactly, but less grim. 'OK,' he says. 'Time for us to go.'

At the back door, Dad embraces Yusuf's grandfather.

'Thank you,' says Dad.

'God protect you all,' says Yusuf's grandfather.

Bibi is looking worried. I can see she's thinking that people don't usually say 'God protect you' to people who are going to a safe place. I'm about to whisper to her that it's just a saying, then I remember there's something else I have to do.

I turn to Yusuf. This is the moment I've been dreading, but I have to do it. I hold out my football.

'This is yours now,' I say.

Yusuf shakes his head.

'Yes,' I say. 'I took your ball and got it blown up. It's only fair.'

Yusuf shakes his head again. 'Where you're going,' he says, 'you'll need it.'

'After tomorrow we don't know where we're going,' says Bibi.

'That's why you'll need it,' says Yusuf.

I put my arms round him. I've never done this before to a kid who's not my sister, but it's the only way I can say thank you. If I try and talk, I'll cry.

'I'll miss you,' says Yusuf.

I nod so he knows I'll miss him just as much.

'Come on,' says Dad.

We creep out the back door.

'Thanks for all the football on TV,' I call softly to Yusuf's grandfather. He gives me a wave.

'Hope they have satellite TV wherever you're going,' whispers Yusuf from the doorway.

'Thanks,' I whisper.

'Shhh,' says Dad.

The three of us scurry down the dark alleyway and get into the taxi. Dad makes me and Bibi lie on the floor in the back.

'Jamal,' says Bibi into my ear as Dad starts the engine. 'Why isn't Mum with us?'

I think about this.

'She's still got more school parents to warn,' I whisper. 'Explain to them why our house was blown up and tell them to be careful and give the kids homework for while we're away.'

That sounds right. With ancestors like hers, Mum isn't going to let an exploding house put her off her duty.

'After tomorrow,' whispers Bibi, 'we'll all stay together, won't we?'

I try not to think about the government wanting to kill us.

'Yes,' I say. 'Whatever happens, this family will always be together. We may not be in Manchester, but we will always be united.'

It sounds corny, but my heart is thumping, that's how much I want it to be true.

11

I wake up.

My neck is stiff and my eyes hurt in the sunlight and I've got breadcrumbs stuck to my face.

I'm still on the floor of the taxi. Bibi is asleep on the back seat. Her head is on her arm and she's dribbling. I gently wipe the dribble off her chin with my sleeve. It's what Mum would do.

I kneel up and peer out the window.

Dad is steering the taxi off the road. We bump over some potholes and stop under a row of trees.

'Are we there yet?' says Bibi sleepily.

I hope not.

In the distance, past the trees, I can see the roofs of city buildings. I don't know much about city buildings because I've only been to the city twice in my life, but I do know one thing. City buildings often have the government in them.

'Good morning, you two,' says Dad.

'Is Mum here?' I ask anxiously.

Dad takes a moment to answer.

'Not yet,' he says. 'She'll be along a bit later.'

'How much later?' says Bibi.

Just for a second I think Dad is going to lose his temper. The tops of his ears go pink, which is always a dangerous sign for certain members of this family. But he just swallows and looks determined.

'I'm not sure exactly what time she'll be here,' he says. 'But she will. I promise.'

That's all I need to hear. In our family we always keep promises. Mum's probably getting a lift from one of the other school families. Mussa's parents have got a motorbike.

We all get out and stretch our legs.

I glance up at the trees. Their fronds are rustling in the breeze. I think how lucky city people are. Living in the country we don't have trees.

Except, I see now, these aren't real trees. They're actually light poles with huge straggling bunches of tangled cassette tape hanging off them. In among the flapping brown strands I can see empty music cassettes. I know what they are because Yusuf's grandfather has some. He loves Dolly Parton.

Dad sees me looking.

'Tape trees,' he says. 'The government hates music, so they confiscate tapes from motorists and chuck them up there as a warning.'

Dad stares up at the ruined tapes. For a moment I think he's going to climb up and rescue them, but he doesn't.

'That's why I taught you to whistle,' he says. 'So you can annoy the government whenever you want.'

I give Dad a grin. He tries to grin back but his eyes won't go along with it. Poor thing. He's been awake all night.

Early morning traffic zooms past us towards the city. Suddenly I have a scary thought. What if a passing government employee from the illegal schools department recognises Dad?

I try to stand between him and the road.

'Come on,' says Dad. 'Let's get you two settled down.'

I'm not sure what he means. He grabs the bags from the taxi and leads us through the tape trees to an abandoned shop. I can tell it's a shop from the big faded Coke and Fanta signs on the front. Dad has told me about the days before fizzy drinks were banned.

The shop door is hanging off and inside it's a bit messy. On the floor are old campfires that have gone out. And tattered pieces of cardboard. The type that people without houses sometimes sleep on.

'Sorry it's not cleaner,' says Dad. 'But you'll be safe here till I get back.'

I stare at Dad. 'Are you leaving us here?' I say.

'You're not,' says Bibi, outraged. 'You're not leaving us here.'

Dad hugs us both. It almost feels like he's more scared than we are.

'I've got to go and pick Mum up,' he says. 'It's better if you two wait here.'

'Why?' demands Bibi.

That's what I want to ask too.

Why can't Mussa's parents drop Mum here?

But I don't. Because from Dad's face I can see there's something we don't know. Something scary and dangerous. Something that makes Dad want to keep me and Bibi safely hidden away here. And I'm scared to ask.

Dad kisses me and Bibi on the head. 'There's breakfast in that bag,' he says, trying to sound cheery. But his voice is trembling. 'I won't be going far. The football stadium's just over there.'

The football stadium?

Dad is pointing out of the shop, past the tape trees. In the distance I can see the top of a curved mudbrick wall.

That must be it.

The football stadium.

The one place in the city I've always wanted to visit.

Dad suddenly drops his arm as if he hadn't meant to mention the football stadium.

'Bibi,' he says. 'Can you get the breakfast things out?'

Then he steers me out of the shop.

He hands me a folded piece of paper and a wad of money.

'This is in case I'm not back here by late this afternoon,' he says softly, glancing over his shoulder to make sure Bibi can't hear. 'Find a taxi, give the note and the money to the driver and he'll take you both back to the village. But I will be here, I promise.'

I've never held so much money. I'm still staring at it when I realise Dad's in the taxi and driving off.

I wave, but I don't think he sees me. Then I stuff the money and note into my pocket and go back into the shop.

'Let's have breakfast,' I say to Bibi. I don't say anything about the money. I don't want her to be worried. One of us is enough.

'If Dad doesn't come back,' says Bibi, 'we're going to use that money to buy a tank and blow up whoever's hurt him and Mum.'

Little sisters, they see everything.

I can see she's struggling not to cry. While we eat I try and cheer her up with stories of some of the best goals I've seen. She's not very interested, not even in the one where a West Ham striker slipped over and grabbed wildly at something to stop him falling and accidentally pulled down the Arsenal goalie's shorts.

I'm not very interested either. All the while I'm talking, I'm not really thinking about golden goals. My mind's somewhere else.

The football stadium.

Why is Dad picking Mum up there?

'Jamal,' complains Bibi. 'Your yoghurt's dripping on my leg.'

Suddenly it hits me. I know why Mum and Dad are going to the football stadium. They've got the same plan as me. They're going to talk to a government football official about me and Bibi. They're going to explain how our football skills will help Afghanistan have a national team one day. So the government won't want to kill us any more.

That happens in families, people having the same idea. Bibi and I both gave Mum blackboard dusters for her birthday last year.

'This is fantastic,' I say out loud.

'It's only yoghurt,' says Bibi.

I explain to her what Mum and Dad are doing. I can hardly get the words out, I'm so excited. Bibi is doubtful at first, until she realises she's in the running for the national team too.

'Fantastic,' she says, eyes wide.

Another thought hits me. One that makes me jump up and spill the rest of the yoghurt.

If Mum and Dad are really going to convince that government football official, they need us there too.

12

People are milling around outside the football stadium. Hundreds of them. They seem pretty excited. But not as excited as me.

'There must be a match,' I say to Bibi. 'The government must have given permission. This is great. The national team selectors could be here.'

Mum and Dad, you are so clever.

I smile as I imagine how delighted the national team selectors will be to meet us. Their job must be so boring, never selecting anybody.

Bibi looks doubtful. 'I don't think I'm ready for national selectors,' she says. 'I've only ever scored one goal outside my bedroom.'

'You'll be fine,' I say. 'It's talent they're looking for in a nine-year-old, not experience.'

I give her the ball to hold while I tuck a few strands of her hair back under her hat. It's actually Dad's hat, so it's a bit big.

'Remember you're meant to be a boy,' I tell her.

'We won't show them you're a girl till after you've dazzled them with your ball skills.'

'These pants of yours are really loose,' grumbles Bibi. 'I can hardly walk in them, let alone play football.'

There are quite a few taxis pulling up outside the stadium. We push through the crowd, looking for a red one with a green driver's door and a photo of me and Bibi hanging from the mirror.

No luck. Mum and Dad don't seem to be here yet.

'We'll never find them,' says Bibi, pulling my pants up and squinting through the dust.

'Keep looking,' I say.

I explain to her that this stadium is nowhere near as big as the ones on TV, but it can still probably hold two thousand people. That's at least two hundred taxi loads. There'll be plenty more taxis arriving before the match starts.

'What if they've parked the taxi?' says Bibi. 'What if they're in the crowd?'

It's a good point. We push through the throng, searching for two familiar bodies.

Still no luck.

Bibi cups her hands round her mouth. 'Mum, Dad, where are you?' she yells at the top of her voice.

I grab her and pull her through the crowd, away from the staring faces.

'Bibi,' I plead. 'We don't want to attract quite so much attention. Just the selectors, OK?'

I can't believe it. Some people just don't know

59

how to behave when they're on a government death list.

Then I see something amazing. The stadium gates are open. People are just walking in without tickets. There aren't any ticket collectors. Either they haven't arrived yet because they couldn't get a taxi, or this is a free match.

'Come on,' I say to Bibi. 'Let's look for Mum and Dad inside.'

The stadium is almost full. It must be a big match. Maybe a famous club is on tour. Real Madrid or Juventas. Or even Manchester United. Sir Alex Ferguson could be in the dressing room right now, giving his players a stirring speech and checking their hamstrings.

'Let's go up to the high seats,' I say to Bibi. 'We'll be able to spot Mum and Dad better from up there.'

We push our way up the crowded steps to the very back row of seats, right up the top, ten or twelve rows from the pitch. While Bibi peers around at the spectators, I lean back over the stadium wall and check out the people and taxis around the entrance.

Except there aren't many people left outside. And hardly any taxis.

Suddenly the whole stadium goes quiet.

For a panicked second I think it's because they've recognised me and Bibi as students from an illegal school. I put my arm round Bibi. But it's not that. An army truck has driven onto the pitch.

I'm shocked. Don't they realise that heavy vehicles

can damage the playing surface? It's really hard to dribble through tyre ruts. I know, I've tried. If Sir Alex Ferguson sees them, he'll go mental.

The truck drives to the far end of the pitch, stops, and soldiers jump out. They open the back of the truck and drag out several women. Even at that distance I can tell they're women because they're covered with clothes from head to foot.

What's going on?

'Look,' whispers Bibi. 'Their hands are tied up.'

She's right.

The soldiers start chaining a couple of the women to the goal posts.

Suddenly I understand what's happening. It's a warning from the government. The women are pretending to be football players. The government is showing what will happen to women who play football.

I feel Bibi stiffen as she realises this too.

Part of me wants to run onto the pitch with Bibi and show the crowd her football skills so they'll see how stupid the government is.

But another part of me is starting to think this isn't such a good idea. The soldiers have got guns. Even though this is just pretend and the guns probably aren't loaded, they could still give you a nasty whack around the head.

I can tell Bibi feels the same. She's shaking.

'Jamal,' she whimpers.

I hug her closer.

Suddenly one of the women breaks away from the soldiers and runs towards our end of the pitch. All the spectators in the stadium start yelling at her. They yell angry, rude, nasty things. The people around me are getting really worked up. The noise makes my head hurt. I put my hands over Bibi's ears.

I can't take my eyes off the woman.

There's something about the way she's running.

No, it can't be.

No, don't let it be.

Lots of women have clothes like that. Lots of women run like that. The exact way Mum used to run when Bibi was a toddler and we had family walks in the desert and Bibi made a break for it.

'Mum,' whimpers Bibi. 'It's Mum.'

It is.

It's Mum.

Down there on the pitch. Hands tied. Running from soldiers. This isn't pretend. This is real.

I stare, numb with shock, trying to take it in, as two soldiers catch Mum at our end of the pitch and fling her to the ground. They point their rifles at the back of Mum's head.

The stadium goes silent.

'No,' screams Bibi.

I clamp my hand over her mouth. People glance at her, then turn back to the pitch.

'It's just a warning,' I plead into Bibi's ear. 'They're just warning Mum not to run away.'

But why? Why is Mum here?

Suddenly I realise. Last night. The government must have arrested Mum before they blew up our house. These women must all be illegal teachers, here to be punished.

Oh no.

Up the other end of the pitch the soldiers are making the other women kneel down. Pointing guns at the backs of their heads too. Taking aim.

I try to scream but all that comes out is a horrified sob.

They can't. The government can't do this. They can't kill people for being teachers.

'Mum,' whimpers Bibi.

'Stay here,' I say to her.

I stuff the ball and Dad's money into her hands and fling myself down the stadium steps. I don't know how I'm going to do it, but I've got to stop them shooting Mum.

Other people are running down the steps too. One of them is Bibi, I can hear her sobbing behind me. For a moment I think the other people are going to help me. But they don't run onto the pitch, they run out of the stadium. They don't want to save Mum, they just don't want to see her shot.

It's just me and Bibi.

Then I hear shouting from the stadium entrance, and the screeching of tyres. A taxi is speeding into the stadium. It smashes through the low fence round the pitch.

People scream.

Smoke is pouring from the back windows of the taxi as it hurtles past Mum and the two soldiers.

It does a half-circle in front of the other soldiers at the far end of the pitch, spraying them with grit. Burning oil cans fly towards them out of the driver's window. The soldiers dive for cover.

The taxi accelerates out of the smoke and speeds down the pitch towards Mum.

The two soldiers with Mum aim their guns at the taxi. Mum scrambles up and starts running again. The taxi goes into a broadside skid and slams into the two soldiers, sending them sprawling, their guns sliding away across the pitch.

The passenger door of the taxi flies open. Mum sees this, runs to the taxi and flings herself in.

People are shouting. The stadium is full of smoke. I can just make out the soldiers at the other end of the pitch stamping on the burning rags from the oil cans and aiming their guns towards the taxi. People are crawling under their seats.

Gunshots crackle. I'm so numb with shock I can't move. The taxi wheels spin. The taxi lurches forward. For a moment it looks like it's going to crash into the goalposts at this end. Then it veers away and hurtles across the pitch and out of the stadium.

I struggle to breathe.

Bibi is clutching me, struggling to speak.

'Jamal, it was . . . it was . . .'

It was.

It was Dad.

13

We're out of the crowds now and almost back at the shop. It's taken a while because you keep bumping into things when you're running and crying at the same time.

'Will they be OK?' sobs Bibi.

She's been asking me the whole way, but I don't blame her. I've been asking myself the same thing.

'They'll be fine,' I say to her. 'Dad rescued Mum. You saw him.'

I don't say anything about government road-blocks and helicopters with telescopic sights. I just glance at the sky and feel sick with worry.

We arrive back at the shop.

Mum and Dad aren't there.

Bibi howls. I hug her and hug myself at the same time. 'This is good,' I say to us both. 'If they got back first and found we weren't here, they'd be really worried.'

I wish it felt good.

'But why aren't they here?' wails Bibi.

'Dad probably wants to make sure he's not being followed,' I say, desperately hoping I'm right. 'He's probably whizzing down one-way streets the wrong way, you know, like he's told us city taxi drivers do.'

I decide to pack our bags to be ready for a quick getaway when Mum and Dad do arrive. I go into the shop, then remember I packed everything before we went to the stadium. Everything except my ball, which I pack into my rucksack now.

And Mum's candlestick, which we left with a candle burning in it. The candle is still burning. I'm not going to pack that. Not yet.

'Jamal.'

It's Bibi, screaming.

I rush outside. A vehicle is speeding off the road in a blur of red and green. It ploughs across the open land and stops in a whirl of dust between the tape trees and the shop.

Now I'm screaming too, we're both screaming their names as we run towards the taxi.

Mum and Dad get out.

We cling on to each other, all four of us, so hard it feels like my arms will snap. Then Dad pulls away. 'We've got to move fast,' he says, going to the boot of the taxi.

I'm not ready to move fast, but Mum pulls away too.

'I thought they were going to kill you,' sobs Bibi, clinging to Mum's dress.

'No', says Mum softly, stroking Bibi's head.

Then Mum stares at Bibi as she realises we were in the stadium. She looks at me. I nod. No point in hiding it.

'Were they going to kill you because you're a teacher?' says Bibi.

Mum looks away. She nods. Her face is pale and dazed. Suddenly I can see she thought they were going to kill her too, and that makes me cry again.

Mum turns and moves towards the shop. She stops. She stares at the candle burning in her candlestick. She turns back and puts her arms round me and Bibi again.

'Thank you,' she whispers.

'Mum,' says Bibi in a tiny voice. 'What will happen to those other women?'

Mum doesn't say anything for a long time. I look up and see the anguish on her face. My own chest hurts with the sadness of it.

'We couldn't do anything,' I say softly to Bibi. 'We're just a family.'

Mum takes a deep breath. 'And we're going to stay a family,' she says, keeping her arms round us. 'No matter where we go.'

She's never held me so tight.

'Are we going on a trip?' asks Bibi.

Mum nods.

'Where?' asks Bibi.

'A long way away,' says Mum.

'Like a holiday?' asks Bibi.

Mum hesitates. Then she gives me and Bibi a brave smile.

'Sort of,' she says.

'When are we going?' asks Bibi.

'Very soon,' says Dad from over by the taxi.

I turn and see he's crouching by the driver's door with a can of paint. He's already painted half the green door red. He takes a lump of chewing gum out of his mouth and pushes it into a bullet hole and paints over it.

'Come on Bibi,' says Mum. 'Let's get the things in the car.' She goes into the shop. She's incredible. An hour ago she was nearly shot and now she's organising Bibi.

While Dad paints, I kneel next to him and catch the drips off the bottom of the door with my sleeve. The government will be on our trail soon and we don't want to leave tracks.

'Clever thinking, Jamal,' murmurs Dad.

That makes me feel good.

'Dad,' I say. 'What you did was so brave, driving into that stadium and rescuing Mum. But I wish you'd taken us. We could have helped you throw the smoke cans.'

Dad stops painting and stares at me. I remember he doesn't know I was in the stadium. I swallow. He puts a paint-spattered hand on my shoulder.

'Jamal,' he says quietly. 'You are a part of my heart and a part of my soul. I'm proud that you're my son.'

I put my arms round him so he can feel how I'm glowing inside.

'I'm proud that you're my dad,' I say.

We look at each other. And suddenly I know that if Dad can be a desert warrior in a football stadium, so can I.

Then I remember we have to move fast.

'Shall I scratch the boot?' I ask. 'And put some dents in the back doors? To disguise it more?'

Dad blinks. He gives a flicker of a smile and shakes his head.

'This'll be enough,' he says. 'It's just to get us to the other side of the city. Then I'm going to sell the taxi to get money for our trip.'

I look at Dad in amazement.

Sell the taxi?

That must be really sad for him. He's had that taxi for years. Longer than he's had me and Bibi. We must be fleeing to somewhere too far away to go in the taxi. Somewhere up some really steep hills. The taxi was never that good at hills.

While Dad finishes the painting, I catch the drips and keep an eye out for government trucks and try not to think about the other women in the stadium.

Mum sticks her head out of the shop.

'If you want to go to the toilet,' says Mum, 'go now.'

None of us do.

I'm too busy having thoughts about my new plan.

'If a person goes somewhere else and becomes a huge football star,' I say to Yusuf's grandfather in my imagination, 'and so does his sister, and they play regularly on TV, and then they come back to Afghanistan with their parents, do you think they'd be popular enough to help form a new government? A kind and fair government that wouldn't murder anyone?'

'Yes,' says Yusuf's grandfather.

He's pretty old and wise, Yusuf's grandfather, even in my imagination, and he knows about these things.

'OK,' I say to him, 'I'll do it.'

14

'Mum,' groans Bibi. 'Are we there yet?'

Mum doesn't reply for a while. In the darkness I can feel her taking a deep breath and trying to stay calm. This is the millionth time Bibi has asked.

'No dear,' says Mum. 'Be patient.'

It's hard being patient lying here under these smelly old sacks in the back of this lurching, noisy, cold truck. I know it's a mountain road, but you'd think the driver could manage to avoid a few of the potholes. Specially as he's been paid all the money Dad got for the taxi.

'Ow,' says Bibi. 'My knees hurt.'

'Here,' says Mum, rustling in the dark. 'Have another lolly.'

I'm tempted to nag Mum and Dad myself. These sacks are really itchy. They smell like they've had goats in them. And I wouldn't mind another lolly. But I don't say anything. Bibi needs the lollies more than me. And we all need to be under the sacks in case a government patrol stops the truck.

'I want to do a wee.'

'Bibi,' says Mum crossly. 'I told you to go before we left.'

'We can't stop now, flower,' says Dad. 'You'll just have to wait.'

The truck hits a big hole. I wish it wouldn't do that. All this jolting is making my bladder feel full too. I have to get my mind off it. I decide to ask the question I've been too scared to ask.

'Dad,' I say. 'Where exactly are we going?'

I've wanted to ask since we left the city, but I've been worried about what the answer might be. I so much want it to be somewhere that has a famous football team. Like Barcelona. Or Brazil. Or Manchester.

Dad isn't answering. Perhaps he's concentrating on his bladder muscles. I feel Mum reach over and touch Dad.

'I think we should tell them,' she says.

'All right,' says Dad.

He goes silent again. For a second I wonder if he's forgotten where we're going, but he hasn't. When I hear his voice again I realise he needed that bit of time to control his emotions.

'Mum and I have decided,' he says, 'that we should all live as far away as we can from the government. We've decided to try and go to Australia.'

Australia?

If my chin wasn't on the floor of the truck, my mouth would be falling open. And if my chest wasn't on the floor too, my heart would be sinking even further than it is now.

I'm not even sure where Australia is. If we did Australia in geography at school, I must have been daydreaming about football at the time. I think it's a big place down the bottom of the globe somewhere. All I know for sure is that Australia hasn't got a team in the English Premier League.

'Where's Australia?' says Bibi.

'A long way away,' says Dad, and in his voice I can hear how much he wishes we could stay at home.

'Australia is a wonderful place to start a new life,' says Mum. Her weary voice is struggling not to sound sad, but it does. 'People in Australia are safe and happy. And it's too far away for the government to find us.'

Suddenly the truck gives a huge lurch and starts to slow down.

It stops.

I can hear men's voices shouting.

'Lie still,' whispers Mum. 'Not a sound.'

Luckily the truck engine is still rumbling and the sides of the truck are still rattling, so the men outside can't hear the air strikes going on inside my chest.

Mum's hand feels its way to mine and squeezes gently. It helps. I hope she's doing the same for Bibi.

Outside, the men are having a conversation with

the driver. I can't hear everything they're saying, but money is mentioned a fair bit. Nobody mentions opening the back of the truck and shooting the sacks, but some of them are probably thinking about it.

I reach over with my other hand and grip on to Dad's.

We lie here, waiting, terrified.

Then one of the men thumps the side of the truck.

I pray they're not trying to break in.

I pray it's just a signal to the driver.

Suddenly the truck jolts and moves off, the engine whining as the driver changes gears.

I start breathing again. Even though the air is freezing, our hands are all hot and sweaty. Dad holds on to mine for a long time.

'Goodbye,' he says finally, in a choking voice.

At first I think he's saying it to me. Then I realise we must have crossed the border and he's saying it to our country.

Mum starts to sob quietly. Dad lets go of my hand to comfort her.

I feel like crying too, but instead I reach out and touch my rucksack. I want to check that my football is still packed safely. Just because I've never heard of any Australian football teams doesn't mean there aren't some good ones. I want to get all the practice I can on the way there, so I'm ready.

The ball feels fine.

My hand brushes against Mum's rucksack. I can feel the candlestick inside.

'Thanks,' I whisper to Mum's ancestors. 'I won't let you down.'

15

This is the biggest crowd I've ever seen, including the European Cup Final on TV. Even the World Cup Final probably doesn't have as many people as this refugee camp.

Or as much dust.

I've looked everywhere for a football pitch, but there isn't one.

Just tents. Thousands of them. Everywhere you look, all over this scorching hot patch of desert, there are tents made of old plastic or cardboard or twigs or cloth.

We haven't got any plastic or cardboard so we're using Dad's coat for ours, propped up on some sticks. We can't all fit under it at once so we have to take turns. Mum and Bibi are asleep in there at the moment, which is good because it gets them out of the sun for a while.

Dad's off trying to find out how we can get to Australia. I've been trying too. Three days we've been here and I've asked loads of people and not one of them knows. Either that or they think I'm just playing around. People don't take kids seriously sometimes, even in refugee camps.

Oh well, at least I've got plenty of time to practise my ball skills.

Foot, knee, head, foot.

'Wanna buy some water?'

It's a boy with a gloomy face and a plastic bottle.

'No thanks,' I say.

Ever since we got to this camp, people have been trying to sell us things. Water. Food. Old clothes. Or buy things from us. There are pawn-brokers everywhere, giving people money for their possessions so they can buy stuff they need. Luckily Mum's good at packing so we didn't need to buy anything. Except the sticks for the tent.

'Only fifty cents American,' says the boy, pushing the dusty bottle at me. 'This isn't washing water, it's drinking water.'

The boy looks like he's been here for a while. He might know how to get to Australia. Apart from his scowl, he looks kind of friendly.

'Want to play?' I say to him.

The boy nods, not smiling.

I kick the ball to him.

He picks it up and runs off with it.

I can't believe it. He's stealing my ball.

'Come back,' I yell.

I sprint after him.

It's not easy, chasing someone in this place. You've got to dodge trucks, squeeze between tents, jump over whole families and make sure you don't tread on any prayer mats or trip over any goats.

Luckily I'm good at weaving between things. Better than the boy, who sees I'm getting closer. Finally he drops the ball and keeps running.

I pick up the ball.

I'm tempted to try and catch that kid. What he needs is a whack around the head and someone to explain to him about team spirit. It's a pity Yusuf isn't here.

But I don't because of what I see.

I'm in a different part of the camp now. I haven't been in this part before. The tents here are more worn and ragged. The people are different too. Instead of cooking and talking and smoking and running off with each other's footballs like in our part of the camp, these people are all lying down.

Some of them are groaning.

They look sick.

This is terrible. They need help.

What can I do? Mum's got a bit of medicine, but it's mostly for headaches and upset tummies. And it's nowhere near enough for all these people.

I look around helplessly. Through the dust haze, in the distance, I see trucks moving slowly along the camp roads, bringing more people in.

One of the trucks is different from the others. It's white with a red cross on it. I know a red crescent means doctors. I hope a red cross does too.

I race over to the truck.

'Stop,' I yell when I get close.

The truck ignores me. It keeps going. I run after it, overtake it, and bang on its bonnet.

It still doesn't stop.

I sprint in front of it and stand blocking its way. Now it'll either have to stop or run me over.

It stops.

The driver leans out and swears at me.

'Sick people,' I say. 'Loads of them. Over there.'

'Where?' says the driver.

I point.

The driver glances over, then looks at me. 'They're not sick,' he says. 'They're just hungry. We've been waiting a week for a food shipment.'

'Oh,' I say.

Mum's got food too, bread mostly, but for all these people it would only be a crumb each.

'The aid trucks are meant to be arriving any time,' says the driver. 'You look like a concerned young man. Want to help us hand out food?'

'Yes,' I say. Then I remember something. 'If I'm still here. I'm going to Australia.'

The driver looks impressed. 'Australia?' he says. He calls over his shoulder. 'Hey, Gav, someone here you should meet.'

Another man appears from the back of the truck, sits down next to the driver and looks at me.

'Going to Australia,' says the driver, pointing to me.

The other man grins. 'Best country in the world, Australia,' he says.

I stare back. I've never seen anybody with yellow hair, blue eyes and a red nose before. But his voice sounds sort of familiar. Like those Australian strikers who play for Leeds United. This man's speaking my language, but I still recognise the accent. On the front of his T-shirt is a flag I don't recognise. The bit in one corner I've seen before, but the rest is blue with white stars.

He must be Australian.

I'm so excited I can hardly get the words out.

'What's it like in Australia?' I ask him. I hold up my football. 'Are there any good teams?'

The Australian man laughs. 'Soccer?' he says. 'Sure are. Where I come from, Dubbo Abattoirs United are world beaters. They've won the Western District Trophy for the last nine years.'

I gasp. That's wonderful.

'Are girls allowed to play soccer in Australia?' I ask.

'Course,' he says, chuckling. 'Government wants them to. Spends money encouraging them.'

I gasp again. That's even more wonderful. A kind and caring government.

'And are people allowed to be teachers and taxi drivers and bakers?' I ask.

The man grins. 'Definitely,' he says. 'There's thousands of schools and thousands of taxis and millions of cake shops.'

I wish Mum and Dad and Bibi could hear this.

'So there's enough food for everyone in Australia?' I say.

'Buckets,' says the man. 'Supermarkets never close. Even better, if you've got a fishing line you can catch your own tea.'

I'm not sure what this means, but tea out of a bucket sounds good.

'So people in Australia are happy?' I say.

'Happy?' says the man. 'They start laughing first thing in the morning and don't stop until two hours after they go to sleep at night.'

I can see it's true. The Australian man's been laughing right through our conversation.

There's one more thing I need to know.

'Do you have mines in Australia?' I ask.

'My word we do,' says the man.

My heart sinks a bit.

'Lots of mines,' says the man. 'Mines everywhere. Full of gold, some of them.'

Gold?

I stand in a daze as the Australian man gives me a wave and the truck moves away.

Good old Mum and Dad.

Trust them to choose the best country in the world. Even the landmines there have got gold in them so that if you get your legs blown off, you can afford the hospital bills and a wheelchair.

I've got to tell Mum and Dad the good news.

I start heading back in the direction I came from,

picking my way between the tents, but after a while I'm not sure if it is the direction I came from.

I try another direction.

And another.

No sign of our tent.

I ask people, but they haven't seen it either.

Panic grabs my throat when I pass a three-legged goat I've seen before and realise I must be going round in a circles. I start to run, frantic, bumping into people, treading on things. I run for ages till my chest hurts too much and I still haven't found our tent.

Never give up, I say to myself, even when things are looking hopeless.

But sometimes you don't know what else to do.

I'm sitting here on my football in the hot dust, alone in the middle of thousands of people, wondering if I'll ever see Mum and Dad and Bibi again.

What sort of desert warrior am I?

I can't even find my way home.

16

Dad's ancestors give me an idea.

Bread.

If I bake some bread, not only can I feed the hungry people in this camp, but the smell will attract Dad. He can smell baking bread about fifty kilometres away, it's in his blood.

I need flour, and water, and salt, and an oven.

I jump up and look around at the dusty rows of tents. I can build an oven out of dirt, Dad taught me. A kind person will probably let me use some of their flour and water if I promise to give them the first couple of loaves.

But where can I get salt?

When you're fleeing for your life, you don't bother to pack salt. There's probably not a grain of salt in this whole camp.

I squat back down on my football. This is hopeless. I can't even be a good baker. I put my head in my hands. Sweat and tears run down my face and into my mouth.

Yes.

Salt.

Before I can let out a whoop of triumph, a hand grabs mine.

It's not Mum or Dad or Bibi, it's the boy who tried to steal my ball. I pull my hand away, but he grabs it again and drags me to my feet. He's really strong for his size. He must do goalkeeper training. Perhaps that's why he looks so gloomy. Goalkeepers live under a lot of pressure.

'I'll take you to your family,' he says.

'Thanks,' I say. I was right, he is friendly underneath.

'For a dollar,' he says. 'American.'

My heart sinks.

'I haven't got a dollar,' I say, then wish I'd kept my mouth shut.

'OK,' he says. 'The ball.'

I clutch my football tight. But the boy doesn't try to take it. Instead he pulls me by the hand, zig-zagging between the tents. He seems to know a lot of people, judging by the number that scowl and swear at him.

I decide to trust him.

What have I got to lose?

Nothing, as long as Mum and Dad have got a dollar.

The boy leads me out onto one of the main camp roads just as a big modern car drives past.

I wonder why anyone with a car like that would be in a place like this.

The car stops.

The boy gives a yell. 'Come on.'

Suddenly he's dragging me towards the car. This is the first time I've seen him look excited about anything.

'What's going on?' I ask.

'United Nations,' he says.

Two men dressed like English Premier League managers are getting out of the car. People are pushing past us, waving pieces of paper and shouting at the men.

'The United Nations give people tickets out of here,' says the boy. 'Come on.' He flings himself into the crowd, dragging me after him.

I can't believe my luck.

These people can help me and Mum and Dad and Bibi get to Australia. And this kid too if he wants to come. I imagine Mum and Dad's faces when I turn up with the tickets.

'Excuse me,' I yell at the United Nations men. 'I'd like five, please.'

I don't think they can hear me.

The boy has let go of my hand and is trying to wriggle through the crowd to the men. I try and follow, but the crush of people is too strong. There are hundreds now, shouting, pushing, desperate, hysterical.

The United Nations men are trying to get into a

small concrete office. But the crowd won't let them. The United Nations men's clipboards and folders get knocked out of their hands. Bits of paper fly everywhere.

'Excuse me,' I yell even louder.

This is hopeless. They don't even know I'm here. I've got to find a way of attracting their attention.

I know.

Ball skills.

I'll show the United Nations men I can make a contribution to Australian sport and society. They must like football or they wouldn't have United in their name.

Trouble is, I'm being crushed. My ball is jammed against my chest. I can't even get it down to my foot.

'Hey,' I yell at the crowd. 'Don't push. I'm trying to do football.'

They don't hear me.

The United Nations men are yelling at the crowd too, but the crowd isn't listening to them either.

Oh no.

The United Nations men are struggling back into their car. They're managing to get the doors closed. The car is pushing through the mob. It's driving away.

'Come back,' I yell.

It's what everyone else is yelling too.

A few hundred people are running after the car, but they're not catching it. I don't bother. I'd rather use my energy to take a few deep breaths and get over the disappointment.

And come up with a new plan.

Like dropping over to the United Nations place in the morning and doing some ball skills for the men on their way to work. I wonder if that boy knows where they live?

As the crowd goes back to their tents I try to find the gloomy kid but I can't see him anywhere.

I walk for ages.

No sign of him.

I start looking for a good place to build a bread oven.

Then I see it. Our tent, with Mum and Bibi standing outside.

I open my mouth to whoop with joy and relief.

But the joy gets stuck in my throat when I see something else. Something near the tent that Mum and Bibi are watching with anxious faces. Something that makes me sick with panic.

Dad, surrounded by uniformed police.

17

In a flash I see what's happened.

Our government's got spies everywhere. Mum taught us about it in school. I thought she was exaggerating, but now I realise she's right. They must be here in the camp and they've spotted Dad and told the local police to arrest him.

I stand frozen, frantically trying to think how to help Dad. The police all have guns. Any sudden movements could be fatal. But I have to do something because if I don't, Bibi will, and I'd rather have me shot than her.

I walk slowly towards the police, trying not to let fear choke my voice.

'Don't arrest him,' I plead. 'We're going to Australia. Dad won't start another school before we leave, honest.'

The four policemen look at me with narrow eyes.

'Please,' I beg. 'He's sold the taxi so he won't be

tempted to drive without brake lights again.'

Now I'm closer I can see Dad's expression. As I expected, he's giving pleading looks. But not to the police. To me.

I stop, confused. Mum appears at my side and puts her arm round me.

'Jamal,' she murmurs. 'It's all right.'

I turn to ask her what's going on. But I don't because I'm so surprised at what I see.

Mum's face is bare. She's got no clothes on her face at all. I don't think I've ever seen her out of doors with a bare face. I don't blame her. At a time like this I wouldn't be thinking about getting dressed properly either.

Mum is looking anxiously at Dad, and I look back at him too. Just in time to see him give one of the policemen a huge handful of paper money.

Now I understand.

Dad's not being arrested.

He's paying the police not to arrest him.

Thank God.

But where did he get so much money? He must have sold the taxi for more than I thought. The people who bought it mustn't have noticed that one of the doors was green underneath and the back seat smelt of burnt oily rags and the floor was covered with breadcrumbs.

I watch the policeman count the money. The other officers are all watching closely too, in case he makes a mistake. The policeman finishes counting, puts the money inside his shirt, says something to Dad, then walks away with the other officers.

The people nearby are all hiding in their tents.

'I hate those police,' hisses Bibi. 'I hope they spend all that money on dried figs and get the plops.'

I give Bibi a look. I've warned her about insulting referees and this is even more dangerous.

Dad comes over to us, tense and worried.

'Don't worry, Dad,' I say. 'They've gone.'

That doesn't seem to cheer him up, and suddenly I realise why. What if they come back tomorrow to arrest him again? Or the day after? Or some of the other officers down at the police station hear about this and want some money too?

Dad hasn't got any more money.

I stare at my football and wonder if I can sell it for enough money to save Dad. I don't think I can, not even if the pawnbrokers see where I've written 'Manchester United Rule' on it and think it's a genuine Manchester United ball that David Beckham has kicked with his own foot.

I have an even worse thought. What if the government advertises a reward for Dad's death? What if the policemen come back and kill Dad?

Now I feel so tense and worried my head hurts.

Mum puts her hand on Dad's cheek. 'When do we leave?' she says.

'In the next couple of days,' says Dad.

I stare at them. What are they talking about?

'Jamal doesn't know what you're talking about,' says Bibi.

Dad turns to me. 'Those policemen,' he says, ruffling my hair. 'They know people who can get us to Australia.'

It takes a moment to sink in. Then the whoop that didn't come out of me before, comes out now.

Mum puts her hand over my mouth and glances at the other tents. She's probably worried that some of the people who haven't got the money to go to Australia might be feeling sad and unhappy. She's really considerate like that.

I pull Mum's hand away from my mouth. 'You mean we're going to Australia?' I whisper to Dad. 'In the next couple of days?'

Dad nods.

I hug him and I hug Mum. Mum gives me a stern look. 'Stay in the tent,' she says. 'We don't want you running off again.'

I can't hear her at first because a convoy of food trucks is rumbling past. She repeats it. I grab Bibi and take her into the tent and tell her all the great things I've discovered about Australia. Dubbo Abattoirs United and the cake shops and the happy people and the gold landmines.

And the female football players.

Bibi seems a bit overwhelmed.

'I'm not drinking tea out of a bucket,' she says.

'I might have got that bit wrong,' I say.

She looks relieved.

I'm so happy and excited I could play a match for about six hours on a full-sized pitch with teams and everything and not get tired.

Only one thing nags at me.

Why isn't Mum more pleased? I can see her crouched outside the tent talking with Dad. She looks so miserable. Poor thing. It must be how people are for a while after they've been nearly executed. Plus she must be missing her friends in the village. I'm missing mine.

'It must be that,' I say to Bibi. 'Everything's going so well, what else could it be?'

'Some other bad thing we haven't found out about yet?' says Bibi.

I sigh.

Little sisters. They might be good at football, but they're not so good at being cheerful.

18

I've never been inside an airport before.

I saw one on TV once. Liverpool were flying off to play Milan. The players handed their bags in at a big counter and then went to a room with peanuts and drinks to wait for their plane and do leg stretches.

I don't think we'll be going to a room with peanuts and drinks. Our bus driver has just given money to a guard at a gate and now we're driving onto the runway.

That must be our plane parked over there.

'Thank God,' says Mum. So do several of the other people on the bus.

I know what they mean. We've been on this hot cramped bus half the night. I've tried to cheer Mum up with some fond memories of her friends in the village, but for the last few hours it hasn't really worked. She didn't even smile when I told her about Fatima's goat eating Fatima's dad's beard while he was asleep. Usually she laughs quite a lot at that.

'Everyone out,' says the driver.

We all stagger off the bus onto the runway, which is hot under our feet even though it's night.

There's a hot breeze too, and in front of the airport lights Dad looks like a desert warrior with his scarf flapping around his shoulders.

The driver and his assistant fling all our bags onto the tarmac.

'Hey,' says Bibi. 'Careful. I've got dolls in there.'

They ignore her and get back on the bus.

'Excuse me,' Dad yells at them as the bus starts to leave. 'Aren't you coming too?'

The driver sticks his head out of the window. 'You will be met at the end of the flight and taken to the boat,' he shouts as the bus drives off.

Boat?

This is the first I've heard about a boat. Perhaps Australia doesn't have many airports.

Mum and Dad and lots of the other people are staring at the bus as it goes out the gate. Dad doesn't look much like a desert warrior any more. His shoulders are slumped. All the other people are looking pretty worried too.

'I hope we can trust those smugglers,' mutters Mum.

Smugglers?

That explains it. The United Nations would never chew aniseed root and spit inside a vehicle. And they'd certainly never throw people's rucksacks around.

'Don't worry,' I say to Mum. 'They probably just want to get back before their policemen friends have spent all the money.'

This doesn't seem to cheer Mum up very much.

We all stand at the edge of the runway, wondering what to do next.

'Perhaps we should ask somebody,' says a man.

It's not a bad idea, but I can see what Dad's thinking. What would we say? Excuse us, we're being smuggled to Australia, but we don't know where to go next?

'We'll wait,' says Dad.

'I think we should get on the plane,' says Mum. She starts picking up our bags.

Dad sighs. Some men in our village get violent when their wives argue with them, but Dad never has. It's one of the great things about him. That and the camel shapes he can make with his hands.

Dad and Bibi and I pick up the rest of our bags. Other people pick up theirs and we all start walking towards the steps at the back of the plane.

Mum still looks very miserable.

Suddenly I realise what's upsetting her. We've never flown in a plane before. The only planes we've ever seen up close are crashed ones full of bullet holes in the desert.

Mum's feeling scared.

I squeeze Mum's hand. 'Don't worry,' I whisper. 'Our plane won't get shot.'

I don't need to remind her we've got our

candlestick. The precious ancient family relic that's kept us safe from air strikes and landmines and the dodgy brakes on Dad's taxi.

She'll remember once we're on the plane and she can relax.

'Stop!'

An angry voice, yelling across the runway.

Several men in uniform are running towards us. One is holding what looks like a sword, except the blade is a thick loop of wire and the handle's got red lights blinking on it.

My heart stops and I get ready to try and hold them off while Dad and Mum and Bibi run for it. But the men don't grab us, they grab our bags. And one of them starts waving the sword over a rucksack.

'It's OK,' murmurs Dad. 'It's just a security check to see if we're carrying weapons.'

'I'm not,' says Bibi fiercely to a security guard.

One of the guards says something in a mixture of languages and points to a hatch in the side of the plane. I realise he's saying the bags have to go in there.

'No,' says Dad. He doesn't let go of the bag. I know what's worrying him. He's heard too many stories of passengers putting bags in the boots of taxis and never seeing them again.

The security guard looks angry. He says that metal objects in bags are forbidden.

'No metal objects,' says Dad.

The security guard with the sword glares at Dad and glides the sword over each side of each bag. He's just started Mum's rucksack when I remember the candlestick. It's solid metal except for the jewels. Even if she's wrapped it in dirty underwear the sword will find it.

I stare anxiously at the flashing red lights.

But no alarms go off.

The security guards don't jump on us.

Nothing like that happens.

In a way I wish it would. Because this is even worse. This sick feeling I have as I grab Mum's rucksack. And feel desperately for the hard shape of the candlestick. And discover it's not there.

Mum takes her rucksack without looking at me.

Now the sick feeling is really bad. Now I understand where the money came from that Dad gave the police.

Mum sold our candlestick. Our precious ancient candlestick that's kept our family safe for hundreds of years.

'I'm sorry,' whispers Mum.

I know she had to do it. I know it was the only way she could get us to safety. And now I know why she's so miserable.

We're not protected any more.

We're about to get on a plane and place our lives in the hands of criminal smugglers and our ancestors aren't protecting us any more.

19

The plane's taking off.

We should be excited because it's our first flight. We should be delighted because we're safe and together. We should be happy because we're on our way to Australia.

But we're not.

We're just sitting here in silence. Well, not complete silence because the engines are roaring and most of the seats and wall panels and overhead cupboards and light fittings are rattling. But we're not saying anything.

Next to me, Mum has got her eyes closed and in front of us Dad has got his arm round Bibi, but he's staring out the window.

It's still dark outside and there are no explosions or tracer bullets visible so I'm not sure what he's looking at. He's probably having the same sad thoughts as me. About leaving our home and our friends and our candlestick.

To take my mind off the candlestick I try to imagine what Yusuf is doing now. Sleeping probably. Dreaming about the tiny pieces of his football.

That makes me feel even sadder.

When I arrive in Australia I'm going to get a part-time job and buy Yusuf the best football in the world and send it to him. I'll decorate it so the government thinks it's an inflatable prayer mat. And I'll send Yusuf's grandfather some Dolly Parton cassettes hidden in Australian landmine boxes.

What was that?

One of the overhead cupboard doors just fell off. It's all this bumping and jolting. Old planes like this can't take it.

I'm sitting next to a window like Dad, but I'm not looking out. It's too scary, taking off in an ancient plane without ancestors.

Lots of the other passengers sound scared as well. They're praying out loud. I don't blame them. They probably had to sell their candlesticks to buy their tickets too.

I think the crew on this plane were pretty thoughtless before we took off, going on about oxygen masks and lifejackets and emergency brace positions to a bunch of people who are feeling very nervous anyway.

Oooh. As the plane goes up, your insides go down. That can't be very healthy, specially for older people like Mum and Dad. It could strain their hamstrings.

Mum's knuckles are white as she grips the edge of her seat.

I put my hand on hers.

'It's OK, Mum,' I say. 'This plane's safer than it looks. The machine guns and rockets are in secret compartments. If we're attacked, they pop out automatically.'

'It's a passenger plane, Jamal,' says Mum without opening her eyes. 'Passenger planes don't have machine guns and rockets.'

I've got a horrible feeling she's right. I couldn't see any weapons as we got on the plane. And I've looked at the safety card in the seat pocket and none of the drawings show a single machine gun or rocket. I can't believe it. A plane this size must have cost millions. It's a disgrace to try and save a few dollars by leaving off the weapons.

Bibi turns round in her seat.

'It's probably got bombs,' she says.

I sigh. Bibi means well, but sometimes she makes things worse.

'This is a passenger plane,' I say, partly to her, but mostly so Mum can hear. 'Passenger planes don't leave their scheduled flight paths and go off on bombing raids. Not when they haven't got machine guns and rockets to defend themselves against anti-aircraft fire.'

Bibi sticks her tongue out at me.

Mum still has her eyes closed, but she looks a bit more relaxed now that I've put her mind at rest.

As the plane lurches on into the night, I realise this is what we're going to have to do from now on.

With no candlestick to look after us, we're going to have to look after each other.

20

These smugglers are being really unfair.

First they keep us shut in a hot stuffy house for ages with only one meal of noodles a day, and then they keep us standing on this dockside for almost a whole night. They don't seem to realise the danger we're in. One look at Dad's face would tell them.

'Dad,' I say. 'Do you think the government has sent spy planes after us?'

'No, Jamal,' he says, putting his arm round me. 'Don't worry, son. We're a long way from the government now.'

But he glances up at the sky.

I know what he's really saying. We won't be safe till we get to Australia. Then we can relax. The Australian government will look after us. A government that lets girls play football is much too fair to allow bullying.

I can't wait to get there.

The really frustrating thing is, our boat to Australia is so close. Just the other side of that fence.

Boats actually. There are two of them. Which is just as well. There are hundreds of us in this compound. We definitely wouldn't all fit on one. Not with those big fishing nets taking up half the decks.

I wish their wooden sides weren't quite so splintery. They both look like they've spent the last twenty years lying in the desert after a battle.

'Mum,' says Bibi. 'Which one's our boat?'

Mum takes a deep breath.

It's the millionth time Bibi's asked that.

For a second Mum looks like she's going to grab Bibi's headcloth and strangle her with it. Then, because she's a great mum, she remembers we've been travelling for ages and Bibi's only nine and the poor thing's got an itchy rash under her arms.

'Come here, flower,' says Mum. 'Let me blow on it to cool it.'

'They'll tell us which is our boat soon,' says Dad. 'You kids are being great. Be patient a bit longer.'

All around the compound other kids are nagging their parents. They've probably been shut up in houses for days too. 'Be patient a bit longer,' the parents are saying to them. I can't understand all the languages, but you just know. And I can tell from the anxious looks on the parents' faces that they're worried about spy planes like us.

'Dad,' I say. 'Are you sure we'll all fit on those two boats?'

I hope it sounds like a request for information rather than a nag.

'Don't fret,' says Dad. 'It'll be fine.'

But I can see he's looking anxious and wondering like me just how many cabins can fit under the decks of two not very big fishing boats.

Stop worrying, I tell myself. All these families here have paid for this trip. We all had to show our tickets to the smugglers at the compound gate. They're not going to leave any of us behind.

I try to take my mind off worrying by watching the boats bob up and down in the water. I love the way they do that. I've never seen big things floating before. The creaking gets on your nerves a bit, but the bobbing looks great.

And the sea. It's bigger than the desert. In fact in this dawn light it looks a bit like the desert. I'm glad it's not. I'd rather be going to Australia on a fishing boat than a camel.

'Dad,' says Bibi. 'When can we get on the boat?'

'Come on,' I say to Bibi, bouncing the ball on her head before Mum and Dad go mental. 'Football practice.'

There's not a lot of room with so many people standing around, but we find some space and do some passing and trapping.

'Just use the side of your foot,' I say to Bibi. 'No big kicks.'

People are staring at her. They've probably never seen a girl play football before. The kids are wide-eyed with amazement. Some of the adults look shocked.

It makes me very proud of her.

The sad thing is, nobody's joining in. We could have a great game in this compound. Teams and everything.

Hang on, someone else is joining in now.

He's tackling me.

Really hard.

Oh no, I don't believe it, it's the boy who tried to steal my ball in the camp.

I tackle him hard in return, get the ball back from him and flip it up into my hands.

'Hey,' he says. 'That's my ball.'

'No it's not,' I say, gripping the ball tight.

'Is this your family?' says the boy, pointing to Bibi.

'Yes,' she says, eyes flashing.

'Then that's my ball,' says the boy. 'Agreed payment.'

I'm outraged. 'You didn't take me to my family,' I yell at him. 'You went running off after the United Nations.'

Bibi pulls off her headcloth and takes a step towards the boy. Even though I'm furious, I watch her anxiously. When Bibi takes off her headcloth she usually ends up throwing punches.

'Listen donkey-snot,' Bibi yells at the boy. 'That's Jamal's ball. He's had it for two years. See that patch? I helped him stick that on. We cut it out of the back seat of our dad's taxi.'

I hope Dad can't hear us.

The boy is staring at Bibi as if he's never seen a girl like her before. He probably hasn't.

Then he lunges. Not at Bibi, at me. He grabs the ball. I hang on to it. We both pull. He's not stronger than me, but he's not weaker. He can't get the ball from me, but I can't get it from him.

The boy looks over his shoulder at Bibi.

'You can have the ball,' he says to her, 'if you'll be my girlfriend.'

Bibi gives him a look that would scorch the paint off a tank. She hitches up her skirt, runs at the kid and kicks him in the leg.

'Ow,' he screams, and staggers backwards, dragging the ball and me towards him. I fall on top of him. The ball bounces near us. The boy grabs at it.

'No you don't,' yells Bibi and gives the ball a huge kick.

It soars over the heads of all the people, and over the compound fence.

The people all gasp.

The ball bounces off the side of one of the boats and disappears between the boat and the dock.

21

Suddenly everyone around us is moving. For a second I think they're all rushing to get the ball. Then I see that the smugglers have opened the gate to the boats. It's time to get on board. That must be why everyone gasped.

I force all thoughts of the ball out of my mind.

Already people are streaming through the gate and onto the boats. I grab Bibi and push between the people who are still getting their belongings together.

'Mum,' I yell. 'Dad.'

Finally I spot them, trying to wait for us. But they're being carried through the gate by the crush of people. Mum sees us. She points us out to Dad. They hold up our rucksacks and wave frantically at us to come to them.

That's what I try to do.

By the time Bibi and I get through the gate, Mum and Dad aren't that far away. They're struggling against the crowd, which is pushing them slowly towards the furthest boat.

Then Bibi pulls her hand out of mine. 'I'm going to get the ball,' she says.

Before I can stop her, she's squirming through the crowd towards the other boat.

'Bibi,' I scream. 'No.'

I fling myself through the clamouring bodies towards her. By the time I finally reach her, she's lying on her stomach at the edge of the dock, jabbing down into the water with a long stick. She's trying to reach the ball, which is bobbing on the water between the boat and the dockside.

'Leave it,' I yell, grabbing her arm and pulling her up. 'We'll lose Mum and Dad.'

She glares at me tearfully.

'If we lose the ball,' she says, 'we won't get to do the plan. We won't get to be football stars and form a new government and go home.'

I stare at her, torn. Part of me knows she's right, but the other part is desperate to get moving.

'I can make a new ball out of cardboard,' I say, dragging her away from the edge of the dock. 'I've done it before.'

Even as I say it I know it's not the same.

Then somebody snatches the stick out of Bibi's hand.

It's the boy.

'I'll get it,' he says. 'We'll go halves.'

Before I can move, the boy slips over the side of

the dock and disappears.

I drag Bibi to the edge and stare down, horrified.

The boy is crouched inside one of the big tyres that are hanging off the concrete wall. He's reaching down for the ball with the stick.

Is he mad? If the boat bumps into the dockside, he'll be crushed.

'Watch out,' I yell.

'I'm OK,' he replies. 'I've done a lot of fishing.'

Then he slips. He tries to get his balance, but he can't. He gives a howl and tumbles into the water.

'Help,' I scream at the people milling around me. 'There's a kid in the water.'

Nobody is listening. They're all too busy getting onto the boats. Bibi thumps a couple of people, trying to get their attention, but they ignore her.

I look around wildly for a smuggler or a sailor or even a policeman.

Nothing, just desperate people.

There. On the deck. The man in yellow overalls. He looks like a sailor. He's got a long pole with a hook on the end. Perfect for rescuing people.

I grab Bibi and we claw our way through the crush of people and stumble onto the boat.

'Quick,' I yell at the sailor, grabbing his overalls and trying to drag him towards the side. 'There's a kid in the water.'

The sailor doesn't seem to understand.

I shake him.

I yell louder.

I grab the pole.

The sailor scowls at me and snatches it back. Then he slaps me in the face.

I stagger, stars in front of my eyes. Through them I see Bibi kick the sailor. He knocks her down. She grabs his leg and bites it. He picks her up and flings her over his shoulder.

'Bibi,' I croak.

I try to get to her but I'm too giddy and I'm still staggering towards them as the sailor throws Bibi over the side of the boat.

22

'No,' I scream.

I stare down at the churning water. Bibi has vanished already. I drag myself up onto the railing and jump.

The water wallops the breath out of me.

Then I'm under, eyes stinging, desperately trying to see her.

Bubbles float around me in the greeny-gold shafts from the sun and the greeny-grey shadows from the boat and the greeny-pink stars from the smack in the head.

I try to kick my legs and move my arms but the water feels heavier than sand and I'm sinking.

Look for Bibi, I shout silently to myself.

Shapes everywhere. But not Bibi. Just shadows.

Sinking.

Sinking.

A face. Close to mine. It's her. Eyes wide, cheeks bulging. I wrap my arms round her and try to kick.

Get us both back up.

No good. I can't kick hard enough.

Kick, Bibi. Do your big kick.

I can't hold her. My arms won't grip. She's gripping me. My chest hurts. I have to breathe in. Bibi, hang on. I can see Australia.

Ow.

Something's hurting my back.

Something's pulling us up to the surface.

No, don't. The sunlight's too bright. The air's too cold. The rough metal I'm sliding over is hurting my knees.

I can breathe, but I can't see Australia any more.

I'm lying on the deck of the boat. I'm shaking all over. My lips are numb and salty. My knees hurt.

Where's Bibi?

I blink the water out of my eyes and look around frantically.

There she is, on the deck next to me. Coughing. Gasping. Swearing at the sailor in the yellow overalls as he unhooks his hook from her clothes.

He grins at me. I sick up seawater over his boots. He grins even more.

I grab Bibi and hold her so nobody will ever be able to take her away again. Then I close my eyes. I keep them closed for a long time.

I want to go back to Australia.

I saw it. Green football pitches and goalposts of solid gold and little stools for one-legged goalies to sit on. Me and Bibi winning the cup final for

Dubbo Abattoirs United. I was there.

Now I'm here on this deck, shivering. I hug Bibi to warm her up. Somebody puts a coat over us.

After a lot more shivering, I remember Mum and Dad.

I jump up, get dizzy, grab somebody to stop myself falling over, stare around wildly.

'Mum,' I yell. 'Dad.'

People are sitting huddled all over the deck. I look at their faces. They look at me, some sympathetic, some scared. Some of the kids are crying.

None of them are Mum or Dad.

Bibi is on her feet too, shaking my arm.

'Look,' she yells, pointing to the other end of the dock.

It's the other boat. The one that was tied up next to this one. It's pulling away from the shore, heading out to sea. People are sitting all over its deck as well.

Except for two figures, standing at the back, searching frantically among the people around them.

'Mum,' I scream. 'Dad.'

Bibi just screams.

Mum and Dad turn and stare. Mum sees us and puts her hand to her mouth. Dad sees us and starts to climb over the railing at the back of their boat. Mum pulls him back.

Water froths and churns below him as their boat picks up speed.

The gap between the two boats is wider than a football pitch.

Two football pitches.

I stare at them helplessly.

They stare at us helplessly.

Sick panic churns and froths inside me.

'Come back,' I yell at the other boat. 'Please.'

23

I have to move fast.

'It's OK,' I say to Bibi, who's getting hysterical. 'We can radio the other boat and get them to turn back.'

She calms down a bit.

I look for a smuggler to help us.

I can't see any. They must be in that hut at the front of the boat, doing pre-departure checks on the radar and the steering wheel and the radio.

I grab Bibi and we start heading towards the front of the boat, jumping and weaving through the people sitting on the deck. Until someone blocks our way.

The sailor in yellow overalls.

He's not grinning.

'Please,' I beg. 'We're on the wrong boat. I need to tell the captain. Once we get on that other boat you'll never have to see us again.'

Either the sailor doesn't understand or he doesn't care because all he does is spit onto the deck, almost hitting a woman and her baby.

Bibi goes ballistic.

'You slime out of a lizard's bottom,' she yells. 'People like you shouldn't be allowed to work on boats. You're not even fit to work on buses.'

The sailor is starting to look as though he does understand. His eyes narrow and he takes a step towards us.

People scramble out of his way. I can see from their faces they're concerned for us, but they're frightened as well. I don't blame them. When you've been bullied for years by a really mean government, you don't take risks.

Well, most people don't.

Bibi grabs a rolled-up umbrella from a startled passenger and swings it at the sailor's head.

'Donkey wart,' she yells.

I block the umbrella with my arm. It hurts, but I manage to grab Bibi and restrain her. I don't think I'm going to be able to restrain the sailor though. He's coming for us. And we can't get away. We're hemmed in by people.

'Stop that.'

An angry voice shouts from the front of the boat. A smuggler, a big man with hairy arms, is striding towards us.

'Get to work,' the smuggler yells at the sailor. 'Prepare for departure and stand by to cast off.'

The sailor complains bitterly in another language, pointing at Bibi and waving his hands. I hang on to Bibi tight. The smuggler shouts at the sailor in his own language. The sailor scowls and stamps away.

'You should fire him,' says Bibi to the smuggler.

'Be quiet,' snaps the smuggler.

I put my hand over Bibi's mouth and try to look polite.

'Our family are on the other boat,' I say to the smuggler. 'Please, you have to send them a radio message and get them to turn back. If you can't see where they are they'll be on your radar.'

'We haven't got radar,' says the smuggler. 'Or a radio.'

I stare at him. No radar? No radio? What sort of boat is this?

Panic surges through me.

'We have to chase them,' I shout.

'Sit down,' roars the smuggler. 'Be quiet or I'll throw you both off the boat myself.'

Several landmines go off inside me. I can feel Bibi struggling to get her mouth free. But I take a very deep breath and pull Bibi down onto the deck.

The smuggler gives us a hard look and walks away.

Bibi's eyes are bulging with fury. I hold her tight and try to blink my own tears back.

'It's no good,' I say to her. 'If we make them angry, we won't get to Australia and we'll never see Mum and Dad again. We just have to be patient.'

I stare across the water. I can just see the other boat, tiny and almost out of sight. I turn away.

A desert warrior could swim over there and grab

the other boat's anchor chain in his teeth and swim back dragging the other boat behind him. But I'm not a desert warrior. I'm just a kid trying to keep his family in one piece.

After a few minutes Bibi starts to cry, which relaxes her a bit.

'I don't want to be patient,' she sobs. 'I want Mum and Dad.'

'I know,' I say.

'So do I,' says a voice behind us. 'My parents are on that other boat too.'

I spin round. A wet figure with a mournful face is holding something out to me.

'I got our ball,' says the boy from the camp.

I stare at him, guilt flooding through me. I forgot all about him. Someone must have hooked him out of the water too. And he's got my ball.

'Thanks,' I say, shifting over. 'There's a space here.'

'I'm Omar,' he says, sitting down.

Bibi and I introduce ourselves.

'We're being patient,' says Bibi, wiping her eyes. 'Because we'll be in Australia soon and we'll see our parents there.'

Omar stares gloomily at the desert of water between us and Australia.

'If we're lucky,' he says.

24

We're sailing to Australia and things aren't so good.

The deck is very crowded and everyone has to sit squashed together. This makes it a bit unpleasant when people throw up. Luckily they mostly do it over the side.

Omar's been throwing up quite a lot.

'It'll get worse than this,' he says between vomits. 'When the waves get really big, you'll both be chucking too.'

So far Bibi and I haven't. I think it's because we're used to travelling in Dad's taxi. That used to wallow and roll from side to side as well.

'I'm hungry,' groans Bibi, slumping against me.

Poor kid. We haven't eaten since last night and it's late afternoon now. All we've had is half a vegetable tin of water.

I'm lucky. I don't feel hungry because the stink of the diesel engine has taken my appetite away. Plus there isn't any shade on this boat and I've got a headache from the sun.

Most of all, I'm missing Mum and Dad. I never feel hungry when I've got a headache and I'm missing people.

'Not long now,' I say to Bibi.

Two of the sailors are dishing out noodle soup from a metal pot. We've been in the queue for ages, slowly moving along the splintery wooden deck on our bottoms. Now there's only one person in front of us.

There is a problem, though. The sailor with the ladle is the one in the yellow overalls. I'm worried that when he sees Bibi, he might not give her a proper serving.

The person in front of us is completely covered with a dark blanket. They hold out their vegetable tin for some soup. They're not close enough to the pot. The sailor grabs their arm and pulls them closer.

I stare in alarm.

The blanket is dangling in the gas flame under the pot. Nobody seems to have noticed. Flames are shooting up the edge of the blanket.

'Fire,' I yell.

The sailors freeze in shock.

I know why. We're on a wooden boat in the middle of the ocean and there's a gas canister right next to the burning blanket.

I drag the blanket off the person and fling it onto the deck and jump on it until the flames are out.

Bibi helps me. Then I pick the blanket up and hand it back to the person.

And freeze in shock myself.

It's a teenage girl. All she's wearing is shorts and a T-shirt with a sparkly pattern on the front. Her arms are bare. Her legs are bare. Her hair is completely uncovered and sticking out in all directions. She's wearing makeup. She's got black stuff on her eyelashes and her lips are green.

I've never seen anything like her in my life.

The sailor probably hasn't either, because he drops his ladle into the soup.

'Thanks,' smiles the teenage girl, taking her blanket.

She turns to the sailor and holds out her vegetable tin. The sailor looks her up and down, scowls and waves her away. He shouts something at her in a language I don't understand, but I know what he means.

No food.

The teenage girl opens her mouth to protest, but both sailors are waving her away now. The other one does a mime. It's about how people who start fires don't get food.

'Hey,' yells Bibi at the sailor in yellow. 'That's not fair. You're the one who started the fire.'

I groan inside. Bibi's right, but I know what's going to happen now.

The sailor starts yelling even louder and waving me and Bibi away too.

I take a step towards the sailor to mime to him why that's totally unfair. The teenage girl grabs my arm. She's already grabbed Bibi's.

'Please don't,' she says. 'It's not worth it. It's much more important you get to Australia safely and find your parents.'

I take a deep breath. The smell of the soup suddenly makes me feel very hungry.

She's right.

'Thanks,' I say.

'Anyway,' says the teenage girl, her green lips curling as she throws a contemptuous glance at the sailors. 'I bet they didn't wash their hands before they opened the soup packet.'

I like her already.

25

The teenage girl invites Bibi and me to sit on her blanket.

We find a spot easily because all the people around us move back. I'm not sure if it's because they're sorry for us or because they don't want to be sitting too close to a person with bare legs and green lips.

A woman near us offers me her tin of soup. I'm about to take it for Bibi, but then I see the woman has three small children. They don't look hungry now, but who knows when there'll be more soup.

I hesitate, then give the woman a grateful smile and shake my head.

Luckily Bibi doesn't see. She's looking over at the soup pot with a mixture of longing and hatred.

The teenage girl pats Bibi's arm.

'That camel-snot needs someone to teach him a lesson,' says the girl, glaring over at the horrible sailor. 'Starting with the news that yellow is a very unfashionable colour.'

I grin, despite my headache and sunburn.

'I'm Rashida,' says the teenage girl.

We tell her our names.

Bibi looks at her, puzzled. 'Rashida's a boy's name,' she says.

Rashida is tightening the laces of her construction worker boots. 'My brother died when he was a baby,' she says. 'So when I came along I got his name.'

'What horrible parents,' says a voice. 'You must hate them.'

It's Omar, the kid who thinks he owns half my football, back from leaning over the side.

Sadness stabs me in the chest as he mentions parents.

Rashida looks up at him. Her green lips are quivering. 'I don't hate them,' she says, 'I love them very much. They saved for years for this trip, and when they found they could only afford one ticket, they gave it to me.'

She blinks a few times and I don't think it's the makeup getting in her eyes because I'm blinking myself and I'm not wearing makeup.

'Now leave us alone,' says Rashida to Omar.

'Um . . .' I whisper. 'I'm afraid he's with us.'

Omar squeezes himself onto a corner of the blanket and starts fiddling with a bit of fluff. I hope he's planning to collect a large wad of it and stuff it in his mouth.

'Do any of you have anything to eat?' says Rashida.

'No,' I say. 'Sorry. Our parents have got it all.'

Miserably I look at the horizon for the millionth time. Still no sign of the other boat.

'My parents have got it all too,' says Omar.

Rashida unzips a large pink suitcase. She takes out a plastic bottle of water and a can of sardines. She opens the can and gives me and Bibi and Omar a sardine each.

'Thanks,' I say.

I'm starving. I gulp my sardine down. Rashida takes a swig of water and passes the bottle to me.

I want to tell her how I've never met anyone like her before, and not just because all the teenage girls in our village had to stay indoors. I don't in case it embarrasses her. Also I can see Bibi is in trouble. She's really hungry, but she hates sardines.

'Swallow it whole in a mouthful of water,' says Rashida. 'You won't taste it as much.'

Bibi follows her advice.

'Thanks,' says Bibi. 'I'm glad we met you.'

'So am I,' says Rashida. 'You're a nice kid.'

'My sister's really nice too,' says Omar. 'And she can play the nose flute.'

We all ignore him.

'When we get to Australia,' I say to Rashida, 'my parents will repay you for the food, but for now I'd like to give you something.'

I pick up the football.

'Hey, that's half mine,' says Omar.

I show Rashida how I can keep the ball bouncing

from knee to knee while I'm sitting down.

'Would you like me to teach you that?' I ask her.

She grins and nods. 'I would,' she says. 'Nothing like learning new skills to pass the time on a long and boring sea voyage.'

'It won't be boring if we're attacked by sharks,' says Omar gloomily. 'Or whales. Or if a huge storm blows up and giant waves smash onto the deck. Or if a typhoon –'

'Omar,' says Bibi. 'Shut up.'

Nobody says anything for a few moments while we think about what Omar has just said. Then Rashida sits back and bends her knees.

'Come on,' she says. 'Show me how to do it.'

I do, gratefully. Bibi helps me. Bouncing a ball between your knees isn't just a skill, it's a really good way of forgetting about your fears.

For a while.

After a bit, Rashida takes her eyes off the ball and peers at me and Bibi.

'You two are sunburnt,' she says. 'Here, put some of this on.'

She unzips her suitcase and hands me a bottle of sun protection cream.

'I'm sunburnt too,' says Omar.

'Sorry,' says Rashida. 'I didn't notice under all the dirt.'

I'm only half-listening to what they're saying because I'm peeking into Rashida's suitcase. I know it's rude, but I can't stop myself. Our survival could depend on whether she's got more sardines.

She hasn't.

All I can see, in among the clothes, is a big knotted plastic bag of something.

Something, I realise with a jolt of excitement, more precious to us right now than gold or Manchester United season tickets.

Flour.

26

I hope this works.

The sailors haven't stopped me so far, but if things go badly wrong I'm worried they could turn violent.

Luckily the nasty one's asleep. The other three are crowded round me, shining their torches, fascinated by what I'm doing. I don't think they've ever seen anyone baking bread on a diesel engine before.

I've explained to them as best I can with sign language that usually bread goes inside an oven, and that I've made these loaves even flatter than usual so I can drape them over the top of the engine.

Also I want this bread to cook quickly because I've left Bibi up on the deck. Rashida's there, but Bibi will be worried if she wakes up and I'm gone. It's really uncomfortable, sleeping sitting up, and you wake up a lot.

'Please,' I have to mime yet again. 'Don't touch it yet.'

Sailors are almost as impatient with fresh-baked bread as little sisters.

I hope I didn't put in too much salt. It's hard to judge when you're used to the dry stuff. We're in trouble if I mixed too much seawater with the fresh water. And kneading the dough in a plastic bucket by moonlight isn't the best way to get the stretchiness right.

'It's not ready,' I mime to the sailors with even bigger hand movements that I hope don't make them cross.

It was really good of Rashida to let me use the flour. And really smart of her parents to make her bring it in case of emergency.

Talking of emergency, this area here under the deck is awash with water. It's up to our knees. I hope the boat isn't leaking. I've asked the sailors, but they don't seem to know what I mean.

I don't think I'll say anything to Bibi and the others. I don't want to make them anxious. It's hard to digest new-baked bread when your stomach's in a knot.

27

My stomach's in a knot.

'You're a genius, Jamal,' says Omar, chewing his breakfast piece of bread.

I don't feel like a genius, I'm too seasick.

Omar was right. The waves have got bigger. If only the boat would stop going up them and then down them. If only the sea all around us would stop going up and down too.

Bibi clambers over me, back from giving some bread to the little kids. At least she's not seasick, that's one good thing.

'The little kids say thank you,' says Bibi, 'and their mum says you're a genius.'

Omar drags his fishing line out of the water and examines the bait. 'I could be a genius too if these dumb fish would bite,' he mutters. 'I think they know this isn't squid. I think they know it's blanket fluff.'

I groan as the boat moves in several directions at once.

'Poor thing,' says Rashida, putting her hand on my forehead. 'I read somewhere seasickness is meant to wear off after a day.'

'A week, more like,' says Omar gloomily. 'Only five days to go, Jamal.'

I have a horrible feeling he's right. Half the people on the boat have still got it. Some worse than me. All over the deck, people are propped up against each other groaning.

'Here,' says Rashida, adjusting the spare T-shirt of hers she's knotted on my head to keep the sun off. 'Have a sip of water.'

She lifts a vegetable tin to my lips.

'I'm sick too,' says Omar indignantly from under the spare shorts of hers he's got knotted on his head.

Rashida gives him a sip of water too. Bibi gives him a glare.

A whiff of vomit and urine hits me and I struggle to keep the water down.

For the millionth time since we set sail, I remind myself why we're doing this. Freezing on a hard deck all night. Roasting all day. Watching poor little children and old people suffer even more than us.

Australia.

Laughing people.

A kind government.

Mum and Dad and Dubbo Abattoirs United.

I hope we get there soon.

28

I wake up.

I'm stiff and smelly and sore and hungry, but something feels good.

I realise what it is.

I'm not seasick any more.

I lift Bibi's head off my shoulder, careful not to wake her, and gently lean it against Rashida's. Then I stand up and painfully stretch my legs and blink gratefully at the sunrise that's turning the flat sea into a golden desert.

I realise another good thing.

The engine has stopped.

The silence is blissful after three days and nights of rumbling and chugging. All I can hear is the slap of water against the boat and the faint crying of babies.

And, suddenly, a smuggler shouting.

The three smugglers are standing in front of their cabin with the sailors around them.

Noodle soup, I think happily. They're giving us more noodle soup. Except where's the pot?

'There's been a mistake,' shouts the chief smuggler, waving a fistful of boat tickets. 'The price you were charged is wrong. To go to Australia you must each pay another hundred dollars.'

I stare at them, stunned.

All over the deck people are rubbing their eyes sleepily and staring at each other in disbelief. Rashida is on her feet. Bibi sits looking confused, trying to take this in.

The chief smuggler says it again in other languages. People start yelling and wailing. A man jumps up and tries to look at the tickets in the smuggler's hand, but a sailor pushes him down and threatens him with a wooden club.

I see that all the smugglers and sailors are holding clubs. Except the sailor in yellow overalls, who's holding a bucket. My bread bucket.

'Pay the full price,' shouts the smuggler, 'or we turn back.'

There's a lot of crying now, and it's not just babies. I put my arm round Bibi.

The smugglers and the sailors move along the deck, emptying people's bags, thrusting their hands into people's pockets, raising their clubs at anyone who says no. Everything valuable goes into the bucket. Money, jewellery, candlesticks, everything.

I can feel Omar trembling beside me. 'I haven't got anything,' he croaks in a tiny voice.

Nor have I. My pocket money jar got blown up with my room. I pull Bibi close to me and wonder desperately how the smugglers would feel about me teaching them two hundred dollars worth of ball tricks.

I glance at Omar and Rashida.

Four hundred dollars worth.

Not good, probably.

'Fuel is expensive,' the chief smuggler shouts. 'It's six more days of fuel to Australia, only three days of fuel to go back. You choose.'

The bucket appears in front of my face.

'Pay up,' barks the sailor in yellow. Then he recognises Bibi and Rashida. His face twists with dislike.

I duck down and fumble under the corner of the blanket and pull out our last two loaves of bread. I put them in the bucket. I hold my breath while the sailor stares at them. I pray he likes sandwiches.

The sailor grabs the loaves and flings them into the sea.

Before I can offer to make him and the smugglers some fresh bread if they've got some flour, Rashida reaches into her suitcase and hands something to the chief smuggler.

It's a watch.

'Four people,' she says.

The smuggler studies the watch, then tosses it into the bucket.

We all wait for him to say it's not enough. The

134

sailor smirks. Omar prays. Rashida bites her lip. I hang on to Bibi. Ever since the bread hit the water she's been growling and trying to get close enough to kick the sailor.

The smuggler moves on, pulling the startled sailor after him.

We stand here, weak with relief.

When we find the strength to speak, Omar gets in first. 'Where did you get a watch that valuable?' he asks Rashida.

'Dad bought it with the rest of his savings,' she replies. 'He knew this would happen.'

I want to hug Rashida. I also want to hug her dad. Instead we sit here, hoping the smugglers get enough in their bucket.

Finally they do. The boat engine coughs into life and we jolt forward and chug and rumble towards Australia again. I want to hug Rashida and her dad even more.

Instead I stare at the horizon, hoping desperately that if the same thing happens on Mum and Dad's boat, Mum gives up her wedding ring without a fight.

29

'Jamal,' whispers Bibi. 'How many days have we been on this boat?

Her head is heavy against my arm. I open my eyes. The sunlight sears in. I squint down at her face. It's wet with perspiration. She's got a fever.

'How many days?' she whispers again.

I wipe her face with Rashida's spare T-shirt.

'Five,' I say. 'I think.'

'Six,' murmurs Rashida, sitting hunched on the other side of me.

'I was going to say that,' mutters Omar over her shoulder.

I know why Bibi's asking. The food and water on the boat ran out this morning and she's wondering how many days left till we get to Australia. Trying to work out if we can survive.

I've been doing the same.

The answer's three and I don't know if we can.

A lot of the people sitting on this deck look as though they feel the same way. I've never seen so much despair on so many faces.

I wipe Bibi's face again.

'Try to forget which day it is,' I say to her. 'Just try and rest.'

'I don't want to forget which day it is,' says Bibi in a tiny voice. 'It's my birthday.'

I stare at her, my sun-addled brain frantically calculating the date.

She's right.

'Oh Bibi,' I say. 'I'm sorry.'

How could I have forgotten? It's bad enough being stuck out here in the middle of the ocean on your birthday, but to have your own family forget is terrible. I can see from Rashida and Omar's faces that they think so too.

'Happy Birthday, Bibi,' I say to her miserably.

The others do too.

Then I pull myself together. There's not much I can give Bibi for her birthday out here, not even a glass of water, but one thing I can do is try and cheer her up.

'Let's plan a party for your birthday,' I say to her. 'We'll have it when we get to Australia.'

'OK,' she says, brightening.

'My birthday's in four months,' says Omar. Rashida gives him a dig with her elbow.

'In Australia,' I say to Bibi, 'when it's your birthday, the Australian government comes round to your house with a cake and fizzy drinks.'

I'm not completely sure if this is true, but with a kind and caring government it could be. Anyway, it's the thought that counts.

'And sardines?' asks Omar.

'Yes,' I say. 'Probably.'

'And hamburgers with onion and egg and chilli sauce?' says Rashida.

'Definitely,' I say.

'Brilliant,' says Omar. 'What's a hamburger?'

Rashida tells him.

'I prefer ice-cream to hamburgers,' says Bibi. She's looking better than she has for hours.

'In Australian supermarkets,' I say, 'they sell fifty different kinds of ice-cream.'

OK, I'm getting carried away now. The others look at me, frowning.

'Fifty?' says Omar.

'Get real,' says Bibi. 'Twenty, maybe.'

I give them a look to let them know that if I'm exaggerating a bit, it's to make us all feel better.

'What's a supermarket?' says Omar.

Rashida thinks for a moment. 'It doesn't have stalls like a normal market,' she says. 'It's one very big shop that sells everything.'

'Even bait?' says Omar, gloomily eyeing his fishing line.

'Bait and everything,' says Rashida. 'My mum used to love supermarkets.'

'Your mum?' I say, staring at her.

'Didn't I tell you?' says Rashida. 'I was born in Australia.'

Now Bibi and Omar are staring at her too.

'Soon after I was born we had a letter from Afghanistan,' says Rashida quietly. 'Telling us how all my uncles were dead in the war. So we went back to look after my grandparents until they died too. And then the government wouldn't let us return to Australia. My parents are very sad.'

Rashida stares out across the churning water, towards where we've come from. Then she turns away and pulls out her mirror and lipstick.

I watch her make her lips green again, which can't be easy when the boat's rocking and your lips are trembling.

'I'm sorry about your uncles and grandparents,' I say quietly. 'And your parents.'

Before I can stop myself, I'm thinking about my uncles and grandparents. And Mum and Dad.

And suddenly Bibi's birthday doesn't feel so happy any more.

30

The people at the front of the boat start screaming.

At first I think word has just reached them about the fifty different kinds of ice-cream. But when I turn round, I see they're excited about something else.

Another boat is coming towards us.

I jump up, dizzy with excitement myself.

For a wild moment I think it's Mum and Dad's boat. That we've caught up with them and they've seen us and come over.

But it's too big to be Mum and Dad's boat. And as it gets closer, I can see there are no people sitting on the deck. Just a few men in tracksuits and trainers, standing watching us.

Another wild thought hits me. They look like a football team. An international football team, perhaps, travelling to a World Cup qualifying match by boat.

Then I see the men are all holding automatic weapons.

People on our boat are whispering to each other fearfully. They're repeating one scary word that makes my insides go colder than fifty different types of ice-cream.

'Pirates.'

'Oh no,' mutters Rashida.

I realise it must be true. Sailors don't wear tracksuits and very expensive trainers. Football teams don't carry automatic weapons, not even in cup finals.

I pull Bibi to her feet and hold her close. We watch, frozen with fear, as the pirate boat stops next to ours. Several pirates jump onto our deck. The others stand on their deck, pointing their guns at us.

I wait for the smugglers to fight the pirates.

They don't.

Instead, they greet the pirates with big grins. They shake hands. Then they jump onto the pirate boat. The sailor in yellow goes with them. Under his arm is the bucket of valuables.

'They're abandoning us,' whispers Rashida.

I stare in horror. She's right. The smugglers must have arranged this. They've taken our money and now they're dumping us.

'Stinking jackal fleas,' mutters Bibi.

'I knew it,' says Omar gloomily. 'I knew this would happen.'

Some of the pirates are still on our boat. And now something even worse is happening. The pirates are grabbing at the huddled people on the deck. Pulling their coats and blankets off them.

I don't get it. The smugglers have already taken all the valuables.

The pirates are dragging a young woman to her feet. They're carrying her, kicking and screaming onto their boat.

Suddenly I understand.

The pirates aren't looking for money or jewellery, they're looking for girls who are out of doors without their parents. These pirates are as bad as our government.

'Oh no,' mutters Rashida.

I take the knotted T-shirt off my head, pull Bibi's headscarf off and put the T-shirt hat on her head instead, stuffing her hair under it. Bibi understands what I'm doing and knots her skirt between her legs to look like baggy shorts.

'Quick,' I say to Omar. 'Give Rashida your hat.'

'I haven't got a hat,' squeaks Omar. Then he remembers the shorts on his head. He gives them to Rashida.

'Put them on,' I say to Rashida. 'Tuck your hair up.'

While she does, I wrap the blanket round her and rub my hand over her face until her makeup is so smudged it looks like dirt and grass stains.

I signal for us all to sit down. I grab my football and start bouncing it from knee to knee. I knee it to Rashida. She knees it to Bibi. Bibi knees it back to me. I return it, and soon we've got a rhythm going.

I pray that Omar doesn't try and join in. Normally we'd let him, but today his lack of skill could be fatal.

He doesn't.

Not too fast, I beg Rashida silently as the ball goes round the circle. You haven't had that much practice.

A shadow falls over us.

A pirate stops right in front of us, studying the ball as it goes back and forward. I pray he doesn't know how brilliant females can be at football. I pray he assumes anyone with knee skills like Bibi and Rashida must be male.

He's not tearing their hats off and dragging them onto the pirate boat, so it must be working.

Suddenly the pirate grins, takes a step back and swings his foot at the ball.

Even as I see it coming I know I should let him kick it. But my leg responds faster than my brain. I trap the ball and slide it to one side. The pirate's kick misses by a mile and he falls over backwards onto the deck, his automatic rifle clattering down next to him.

The other pirates laugh.

The people around us give a quiet moan.

We wait, frozen, for the pirate to shoot us all.

He doesn't.

Instead he gets up, takes a step back, and kicks me in the hip.

Very hard.

Pain explodes up and down my body. I writhe on the deck, my knees hunched to my chest, my eyes full of tears. For a long time I can't even straighten my legs. All I can do is squint anxiously at Bibi.

Don't attack the pirate, I beg her silently. Please don't.

She doesn't. She wants to, but Omar is hanging on to her as tight as he can and she can't shake him off.

Finally, after Rashida has rubbed my hip for ages, I manage to sit up.

The pain brings more tears to my eyes, but I can still see what's happened.

The pirates have gone.

Their boat is a dot on the horizon.

The smugglers have abandoned us. We're alone in the middle of the ocean, a boatful of starving wailing people and three scared sailors.

This is it, I think. It can't get worse than this.

31

I'm Dubbo Abattoirs United and I've got the ball and everything is good.

The sun is shining.

The grass is green.

The goalposts are solid gold.

Mum and Dad are among the spectators, smiling and waving.

My hip hurts but it doesn't stop me dazzling the cup final crowd with my footwork.

What stops me is Bibi's scream.

Fearfully I look around the stadium. I can't see the problem. There's no army truck on the pitch. No soldiers with guns. Nobody's being chained to the goalposts. And yet I can still hear Bibi screaming.

I open my eyes.

The sky is black. A bitter wind cuts through the huddled people on the deck. Bibi is clutching onto me, screaming into my chest.

I look up and see why.

A huge dark foam-spewing wave is crashing down onto us.

32

I've lost Rashida. I've lost Omar. Bibi's with me but only because our belts are tied together with her headcloth.

We're back to back, scooping with vegetable tins. The freezing oily water is up to my waist. It's up to Bibi's chest. Here below deck we can't see the storm, but it sounds like it's tearing the boat apart.

'This is hopeless,' yells Bibi for the millionth time.

'No,' I yell. 'It's working.'

But even in the gloom we can both see it isn't. This tiny space is packed with people, all scooping, but the water is winning. Every time a wave smashes onto the boat, more water pours in here than we can possibly scoop up in soup bowls and vegetable tins and fling out again.

'The boat'll sink,' yells Bibi. 'We've got to tell the sailors.'

I haven't got the heart to tell her that the sailors are already down here, floundering around under the water trying to mend the bilge pump.

We both flinch as a huge wave crashes into the boat, pushing the back of it up out of the sea. The engine roars and sprays us with hot oil.

'Keep scooping,' I say to Bibi.

It's all we can do.

'How could he,' says Bibi. 'How could that congealed lump of yellow camel-snot take the only bucket?'

Poor Bibi. We're numb with cold. And dizzy with exhaustion and hunger. And so thirsty. This is torture, being surrounded by water and not being able to drink any. It must be worse for her, she's only ten.

I think of Dad's ancestors, countless generations of bakers who got up at 3am even though they needed more sleep and who stuck at it, dragging sacks of flour, kneading dough, twisting their backs to reach into scalding ovens, loaf after loaf after loaf after loaf after loaf.

They didn't stop and I'm not going to either.

I glance over my shoulder at Bibi.

She looks totally exhausted. Even in this faint light I can see how pale she is, hair plastered round her face, scooping with her eyes closed. Her lips are blue.

A lot of the men down here are looking at her. They can't believe a female can keep going this long. They don't understand how she can do it.

I know how.

Her father's a baker.

33

What's going on?

The people up on the deck are yelling and screaming. I can't hear what they're saying because of the engine noise right next to my ear.

They sound terrified.

The people down here have stopped scooping and are climbing up the ladder to see.

I don't want to see.

I don't want anything else to happen. Bibi and I will keep going down here till we drop, but I haven't got the strength for anything else.

I keep scooping.

'Jamal, come and see.'

Someone's yelling at me from the top of the ladder.

It's Rashida. Thank God. She's alive.

'Rashida, come down,' I say.

She doesn't hear me. My voice is too tired to shout. It doesn't matter because I'm moving towards the ladder anyway. I still don't want to go up, but people behind us do and I'm too exhausted to get out of the way so me and Bibi get pushed up the ladder.

We stagger onto the deck and my mouth falls open.

Towering over us, huge, is a warship.

Some of its guns are longer than our whole boat. Plus I can see rockets with armour-piercing warheads. And machine guns with laser sights.

All pointing at us.

People on our boat are panicking. Some of them are grabbing babies and toddlers and running to the railing and holding them up to the warship.

'Don't shoot,' they're yelling. 'There are children on board.'

I'm not panicking.

Even though the warship could blow us out of the water with one press of a button, I'm not scared.

I recognise the warship's flag. It's a flag I've seen before, on the doctor's T-shirt in the camp.

I'm shaking all over. I'm laughing and crying at the same time. I grab Bibi and Rashida to share the wonderful news with them.

'Australians,' I shout. 'They've come to rescue us. We're saved.'

34

There's an Australian serviceman peering into my cabin. I can see him in the doorway, outlined by the light from the passageway.

It's Andrew, I can tell by his uniform and his ears.

When he was carrying me and Bibi onto the warship, and we were all hooked onto the cable and sliding through the air, he could see how scared we were.

'Hang onto my ears,' he said.

At first I thought he'd said it wrong. He speaks our language, but not that well. Then I realised he meant it.

'When God was handing out ears,' he said, 'I asked for handles. Knew they'd come in useful one day. Hang on.'

So we did.

He didn't care if it was hurting him. Australians are like that. Really generous. Also Andrew's an officer, so he's probably been trained to withstand pain.

'Jamal,' whispers Andrew now. 'Are you still asleep?'

'No,' I whisper. 'Bibi is, but I'm not.'

Andrew creeps into the cabin, careful not to trip over the piles of cables and winches lying around. He bends over Bibi's folding bed and puts his hand gently on her forehead.

'Good,' he says. 'Her fever's gone.'

He crouches next to my bed. He's holding a tray with two plates on it.

'Thought you might both still be hungry,' he says, handing a plate to me. 'The speed you ate that first meal, I thought you were going to swallow the cutlery as well.'

He clicks on a torch and shines it onto the plate.

Fish fingers, chips and peas. Same as last time. Andrew says it's traditional Australian food. I love it.

'Thanks,' I whisper.

Andrew's face falls. Suddenly he's looking upset. 'Jamal,' he says quietly. 'I want to say how sorry I am.'

I stare at him, panic turning my first dinner into a hard ball in my stomach. Why is he sorry? Why is he looking so sad? Has he heard bad news?

'Is it Mum and Dad?' I blurt out. 'Has something happened to them?'

Andrew looks confused for a moment. Then he puts his hand on my arm. 'No,' he says gently. 'Don't worry, I'm sure they're fine. Their boat must have taken a different route. We've got a plane out looking and once we've dropped you off on dry land, we'll join the search ourselves. We'll find them.'

Australians are really good at calming you down.

'Or,' I say, 'they might be waiting for us when we arrive.'

'They might,' he says.

I believe him. That's another thing about Australians. You trust them.

'What are you sorry about then?' I say. Another scary thought has hit me. Rashida.

'What I'm apologising about,' says Andrew, 'is the time it took to get you all off your boat. You were cold and hungry and your boat was leaking. We should have done it straight away, but there was . . .'

I can see he's struggling to find the right word. It can't be easy, expressing yourself in another language.

'. . . paperwork,' says Andrew.

'That's OK,' I say. 'I understand about paperwork. My mum's a teacher.'

Andrew smiles, but he still looks a bit upset.

'How's your hip?' he says.

'Hurts,' I say.

'I'm not surprised,' he says. 'The size of that bruise. When I was a kid a truck hit me and I didn't have a bruise that big. I've spoken to the doctor who looked at it. He says it needs to be X-rayed, but we don't have an X-ray machine on the ship.'

I'm not exactly sure what an X-ray is. Probably a traditional Australian method of curing bruises.

I'm sure there'll be loads of X-ray machines around when we land.

'That's OK,' I say. 'Thanks anyway.'

'I'll leave you to eat in peace,' says Andrew.

I don't want him to go.

'Andrew,' I say. 'How come you speak my language?'

'Night school,' he says. 'The navy pays you more if you've got a second language.' He grins. 'Anything else you'd like to ask?'

There are a million things.

I want to know if Bibi and I will be able to go to school at night when we're living in Australia. I hope so, because that'll leave the days free for football practice.

I want to know how to cook fish fingers, chips and peas, so I can make it for Mum and Dad and Bibi.

I want to know where Andrew lives, so if possible we can live close.

But there are even more important things to ask.

'How's Rashida?' I say.

'She's fine,' says Andrew. 'She was a bit dehydrated, so the doctor's got her on a drip, but she'll be up soon.' He smiles again. 'Anything else?'

There is something else. I'm scared to ask because just thinking about it makes me remember the storm and the waves smashing over us and how some people were swept into the sea. But I have to ask anyway.

'Have you found the boy with the football yet? His name's Omar.'

'Not yet,' says Andrew. He gives me a sympathetic look. 'People are scattered all over the ship. I'm sure he'll turn up. And I'm sure your ball will too.'

'It's not the ball I'm worried about,' I say.

Andrew nods. 'I know,' he says. 'Enjoy your meal. I'll leave Bibi's plate on the floor. See you later.'

'Andrew,' I say. 'When it's your birthday and the government brings your cake round, I hope it's a big one.'

'Thanks,' says Andrew.

He looks a bit puzzled as he creeps out. I remember I'm not absolutely sure about the Australian government and birthdays.

After a while I sit up and start eating.

A little later a voice comes out of the gloom, making me jump. 'You can get gut-ache eating too many chips,' it says.

I realise someone is watching me from the doorway. I hear the thump of a ball bouncing on the lino in the passage.

'Hey,' says Omar, coming into the room. 'Is that dinner on the floor for me?'

35

We're in Australia.

Almost.

We're crowded into one of the warship's rubber boats, speeding towards the coastline.

Australia looks so green. Except for the droopy brown palm trees. And the grey buildings with the paint flaking off. And the wooden jetty with plastic bags washed up against it. But the rest of it is really green.

Some of the people in the boat are clutching each other and weeping. I don't blame them. Being here feels even better than I imagined.

But there's one thing we haven't seen yet.

Mum and Dad's boat.

Bibi is next to me, almost in the water with excitement. 'Look,' she yells. 'Is that it there?' She's pointing to a rusty shape at the edge of the bay.

Omar peers at it. I admire his coolness. His parents are on that boat too. I bet inside he's boiling with excitement like me.

'No,' says Omar. 'It's a storage tank.'

I go off the boil. He's right.

I stare up and down the coastline, desperate to see Mum and Dad's boat.

'Jamal and Bibi,' shouts Andrew from the front of our boat. 'Don't lean out so far.'

'He's worse than Mum,' mutters Bibi.

I agree. Australians can be a bit over-protective. We're wearing life-jackets and Bibi's holding a football. If we fall in we're hardly going to sink.

It's just my insides that are sinking.

Mum and Dad's boat isn't here.

Rashida can see how disappointed we are. 'Perhaps it landed in a different part of Australia,' she says. 'Perhaps they're on the jetty waiting to meet you.'

Of course. That's it.

Bibi and I lean out of the boat again and squint at the jetty. I can see quite a few people waiting for us to arrive. They're a bit hazy through the spray and sunlight. Any of them could be Mum or Dad.

When we reach the jetty, Bibi and I are first off.

'Mum,' we shout as we push through the people. 'Dad.'

Nobody replies.

Most of the people on the jetty are wearing uniforms of one type or another. For a wild moment I hope that some kind Australian sailors have lent Mum and Dad their uniforms, but as I study the faces around me I see this hasn't happened.

They're not here.

Panic sweeps through me. My mind does all the things I've tried to stop it doing these last few days. Imagines Mum and Dad fighting pirates. Dying of thirst. Being swept away by a storm.

I struggle to keep the panic and sadness inside me. Poor Bibi's already crying and if I start now everybody could end up distressed. Half the people on our boat have friends or family on the other boat, including Omar.

Andrew comes over and puts his hand on my shoulder.

'We still haven't found the other boat,' he says quietly. 'But we will, I promise.'

I look up into his face and what I see makes me feel calmer. Not the freckles or the red curly hair. The expression in his eyes. I can see that when Australians make a promise, they keep it.

'Cheer up,' I say to Bibi. 'Everything's going to be OK.'

She doesn't look convinced.

I am. As Andrew leads us off the jetty, I feel like running and shouting and scoring about fifty goals.

This is Australia. I'm walking on an Australian pathway. Australian grass is growing nearby. Australian flies are landing on my face.

I hug Bibi. 'We made it,' I say.

She hugs me back and gives a little smile through her tears. 'The grass looks good for football,' she says.

Rashida and Omar catch up with us. Rashida's lips look even greener here in Australia. They're definitely trembling more. She puts her arms round me and Bibi and Omar and squeezes us tight.

'Thank you,' she whispers.

I thank her back and remind her that if she hadn't kept us alive with her flour, we wouldn't have been around to help her with the pirates.

'Neither would I,' says Omar. 'Unless I could have scabbed some food from someone else.'

'OK everyone,' says Andrew when the other people from the boat have caught up with us. 'Welcome to your new home.'

He leads us into a dusty compound. In it are two of the biggest tents I've ever seen. Canvas tents with proper ropes and everything. Inside the tents, Australian servicemen and women are laying out the folding beds from the warship in neat rows.

'Males in that one,' says Andrew. 'Females in that one.'

I feel Bibi freeze next to me. I don't even have to look at her to know what she's thinking.

'No,' I say to Andrew. 'We're staying together.'

Rashida grabs a startled Omar's hand. 'So are we,' she says.

Andrew sighs. He looks at the four of us. 'OK,' he says. 'Just until your folks get here.'

I inspect our tent. It's perfect. It's near the jetty so we'll be able to hear when the other boat arrives. And it'll be great for us all to have somewhere to stay while Mum and Dad are looking for jobs, before we find a house of our own.

Bibi is still looking sad. I have an idea, a way to keep her mind off things.

'Hey,' I say to her and the others. 'Let's explore. Let's go and see all the things Andrew's been telling us about. Shopping centres with fountains. Cinemas with fourteen movies showing at once. Let's go and find an Australian supermarket.'

Bibi is interested. The others are too.

Then I notice Andrew is giving me a strange look.

I realise why.

I'm being really selfish. Mum and Dad and Omar's parents aren't even here yet. At this very minute they could be sitting shipwrecked on a remote island, waiting to be rescued. It'd be pretty mean, rushing off and seeing the sights without them.

I give Andrew a grateful look.

Thank goodness Australians are so good at thinking of others.

36

Bibi kicks the ball to me.

Good pass.

I side-step a tackle from an Australian sailor and pass to Omar. He shoots. Our supporters cheer. It's a good effort, but a bit hopeful from forty metres out. Their goalkeeper runs out and picks up the ball where it's stopped.

'Good attempt, Omar,' I say.

This is a great idea of Andrew's. A football match to keep us occupied while we wait for the other boat to arrive.

Refugees versus Aussies.

I'm having a great time. Bibi is too. Playing with teams is even better than one-a-side. And it's fantastic having a crowd watching. All the people from our boat are here. Even though the warship has gone back out to sea, there are still loads of Aussies cheering their team.

Omar doesn't seem to be having such a great

time. For some reason he's looking even gloomier than usual. Perhaps it's because he's not very good at football.

'Jamal,' he says. 'Have you heard what people are saying?'

Poor kid. He must have heard our supporters criticising his shot.

'Don't worry,' I say to him. 'I wasn't very good at first either. Now we're in Australia you'll have plenty of chance to practise.'

'Not that,' says Omar. 'What they're saying about this camp.'

I can't concentrate on camp gossip. The other team has just scored again. Six nil. These Aussies are so good it's hard to believe they've never played together before today. Andrew reckons they didn't even have a football before I arrived. Which is weird. Why didn't they just go to a supermarket and buy one?

'Jamal,' Omar is saying. 'Are you listening to me?'

'No,' I say. 'I'm not. If you want to win at football you've got to concentrate on the game. You don't see Manchester United gossiping during matches.'

I know I'm being a bit tough, but if Omar wants to improve, he's got to understand the basics.

I hurry back to the centre of the pitch.

'Jamal and Bibi,' says Rashida as we kick off again. 'Run up their end and I'll try and get the ball to you.'

She means play deep striker.

'Me too,' says Omar.

Bibi's off like a rocket. I can hardly keep up with her. Not only can she kick harder than me, I think she can run faster than me. I'll have to train hard or she might get a place with Dubbo Abattoirs United and I won't.

Oh wow. Rashida's done it. The ball's flying towards me. I trap it on my chest and turn towards goal.

My hip hurts.

Two Aussie defenders on me.

Watch this, Sir Alex. I saw David Beckham do this once and I bet you told him about it. Two defenders, go between them, get them confused.

Yes.

It works, and because Aussies are so decent neither of them fouls me.

I pass to Bibi, who's in a great shooting position. Do a scud shot, Bibi. Oh no, an Aussie defender's blocking her. She's not sure what to do. She passes back to me.

I can hear my two Aussie defenders thudding towards me.

'Pass,' screams Omar.

'Shoot,' screams Bibi.

I hesitate, then shoot.

A flash of pain sears out from my hip, but I don't care. The goalie doesn't even move. The ball's like a missile, flashing between the posts, over the crowd and slamming into the compound fence.

I fling my arms into the air.

'Goal,' yells Bibi joyfully.

Our supporters will love this. Nothing like a goal to cheer you up after a long dangerous journey and years of persecution by a vicious and unforgiving government.

Except there's no cheering. Just silence. Our supporters are just standing there, stunned. Some aren't even paying attention. They're having conversations.

Was I offside? Has the referee not allowed the goal? Bibi looks as confused as me. The referee blows his whistle and points to the centre spot.

It is a goal.

Our supporters are making noise now, but they're not cheering. They're wailing and screaming and sobbing.

What's going on?

People are running onto the pitch, throwing their arms round our players, weeping.

My arms are still in the air. I feel the blood running out of them.

Is this something to do with what Omar was saying? Something to do with the camp?

Then I hear what the people around me are saying and I feel the blood run out of my heart.

News has come in about the other boat.

Mum and Dad's boat.

It's sunk.

37

I look wildly around the pitch for Andrew.

We have to get a rescue boat launched.

I can't see him among all the weeping, howling people. Then I remember he's out on the warship.

A group of Australian sailors are leaning against the fence smoking, just past where Bibi is sprawled sobbing on the grass. I sprint over to them, waving my arms.

'Quick,' I yell. 'We have to get a boat launched to go and help search for survivors.'

The Australian sailors look at me.

'Now,' I scream. 'Before it's too late. There are people in the ocean. My Dad can't swim.'

The Australian sailors look at each other. One of them says something to me that I can't understand and waves me away.

I don't believe it. Then I realise what's happening. They can't speak my language. They don't understand.

I grab a stick and draw frantically in the dust. A sinking fishing boat. A warship doing all it can. More people in the water than the warship can cope with, including Mum and Dad.

The Australian sailors stare at my drawing.

This is unbelievable. One of them is actually smirking.

'Don't you care?' I scream at them. 'Don't you care that my parents are drowning? I can't believe it. I can't believe that people can be like this in Australia.'

One of the sailors stares at me. 'Australia?' he says.

He takes the stick from me and draws in the dust. A big island. Then he draws, a long way away from it, a small island. He points to the big island.

'Australia,' he says.

The smirking sailor smirks even more.

The sailor with the stick points to the small island and gestures around us at the football pitch and the tents and the harbour.

'Here', he says. 'Not Australia.'

38

'Jamal.'

Rashida's voice, soft in the gloom of the tent.

I don't look up. I keep my face pushed into my damp pillow and my arms wrapped tightly round Bibi.

'Jamal, Bibi, I've brought you some dinner. It's your favourite. Fish fingers, chips and peas.'

'Go away,' sobs Bibi.

I don't answer.

I don't want food.

I don't want Rashida.

I don't want Australia.

I just want Mum and Dad.

'I spoke to the radio operator here,' says Rashida, her voice trembling. 'The warship did everything they could. After they picked up the three young survivors, they searched for hours. They did try.'

It doesn't help. I keep thinking that if we'd kept the candlestick, Mum and Dad could have lit a candle and the rescuers might have seen them both before they slid down into the depths. Which is a stupid thought because if Mum hadn't sold the candlestick, we'd still be in the refugee camp. Or a government jail.

I wish we were, instead of Mum and Dad at the bottom of the sea and me and Bibi on an island thousands of kilometres from Australia.

I feel Rashida pushing something into my hand. Something flat.

'It's your football,' she says sadly. 'When you scored your big goal, it got punctured on the barbed wire.'

I don't care.

Rashida doesn't say anything for a long time. There's just the sound of Bibi and the other people in the tent sobbing.

I hold Bibi tight.

I hear Rashida take a deep breath. When she speaks, her voice is shaking.

'Jamal and Bibi, I just want you to know that you've still got me. I know it's not the same but you have.'

'Thanks,' I mumble into my pillow.

It feels a tiny bit better, her saying that. But only in the way that the last part of drowning feels better. You still know it's the end, even if you think you can see Australia.

For some reason this thought makes me cry even harder.

When I've finished, Rashida has gone.
It's just me and Bibi.

39

Bibi's asleep at last.

That's why I'm lying out here on the football pitch. So I don't disturb her while I try and plan our future. It's hard to plan quietly when you're crying.

I don't want to think about the future. I don't want to think at all. But somebody's got to do it and Bibi's only ten.

'Jamal.'

A voice out of the darkness. Even though the moon's bright, I can't see anyone.

'Jamal.'

It's Omar's voice, wobbly and uncertain. That's not like Omar. Then I remember his parents were on the boat too. I'd forgotten that. Grief can make you really selfish.

'Over here,' I call to him.

He comes and sprawls next to me.

'I've got something to tell you,' he says.

My first thought is that I don't want to hear. The

170

last piece of news Omar told me here on the football pitch was bad enough. Or would have been if I'd listened. In fact everything people have told me lately has been terrible. Except for Andrew, but he's a liar.

Then I remember Omar is grieving too.

'What is it?' I say.

'They weren't on the boat,' he says.

I roll over and stare at him.

'Who?' I say.

He looks at the ground.

'My parents,' he says. 'They died when I was two.'

Neither of us says anything for ages.

'How did you get a ticket to Australia?' I ask finally.

'I didn't,' he says. 'I hung around a big family in the camp and when they got on buses so did I and people thought I was with them.'

'What about the plane?' I ask.

'Same thing. Hid in the toilet. I'm sorry I lied to you, Jamal.'

Slowly I take this in. Here's a kid with no parents who doesn't let it hold him back. Who goes out and does things. Like travel to Australia without a ticket.

Neither of us says anything for another long time.

I stare up at the stars and think about what me and Bibi could go out and do. We could travel around Australia talking to players whose teams have just lost matches. When we tell them what's happened to us, and they see our tears, things won't seem so bad for them. In return, they might let us train with them.

Omar is fidgeting. I can see he's got something else on his mind.

'Don't ask me about my parents,' he says suddenly. 'Because I don't know anything about them. But I do know about my ancestors.'

'Tell me about them,' I say.

'They were thieves,' says Omar. 'One of them had his hands chopped off.'

I remember Omar trying to steal my football. I also remember him saving it from the harbour. And clinging on to Bibi, saving her from attacking the pirate. Omar might think he's a thief, but it's never that simple.

I give him a look, to show him I know.

'What about your ancestors?' says Omar.

'One lot were desert warriors,' I say. 'The other lot were bakers.'

'Which are you?' says Omar.

I think about this. I think about the things that have happened. My chest fills with grief again, because suddenly I know the answer and it makes me miss Mum and Dad so much.

'I'm a bit of both,' I say.

40

I'm Manchester United. I score a goal. Bibi, who's also Manchester United, gives me a big hug. Mum and Dad, who aren't Manchester United but are there anyway, give me a big hug too. It feels good.

Then I wake up.

It doesn't feel good any more. It hurts a lot. And not just my hip.

Bibi is shaking me. I blink and look around. The tent is full of people shouting and running.

'Jamal,' yells Bibi. 'Get up.'

My first thought is that someone has stepped on a landmine. Strange that. We've been on this island three days and nobody's said anything about landmines. Perhaps they don't want to depress sad orphans.

They don't know me very well.

I've got a plan. Two hours a day crying, the rest of the time being a productive and cheerful Australian citizen.

It can't be a landmine. Those shouts are excited. Almost happy.

'Come on,' yells Bibi. She drags me out of the tent.

People are running down to the jetty.

In the dawn light I see why. The warship is back, sitting in the harbour. I can make out the shape of the rubber boat bouncing across the grey water towards us.

I turn to go back to bed. Then I have a thought. They must be bringing back the survivors. Three teenage boys, Rashida said. Perhaps the teenagers spoke to Mum and Dad while the boat was sinking. Perhaps they've got a message for me and Bibi.

Slowly, limping, I let Bibi lead me down to the jetty.

People are climbing out of the rubber boat. Other people are laughing and crying.

I must still be half asleep. I don't understand who all these people are.

Then I see something that makes me think I'm not just half asleep, I'm still dreaming.

Omar, hugging a tearful family. A big, damp, crying, laughing family.

He sees me and looks sheepish. 'This is the big family I was telling you about,' he says. Then he goes back to hugging them.

I stare. They're real all right.

Next to them a man from our tent is talking to an Australian officer. Suddenly the man crumples into tears and slumps down onto the jetty.

'No,' he sobs as the officer tries to help him up. 'I don't want to live. Not without them.'

My insides start to hurt as I realise what is happening. News must have come back about the people on the other boat who drowned.

Bibi grips my hand and screams.

An ecstatic, joyful scream.

I spin round.

Mum and Dad are standing there.

'The warship didn't see us,' says Mum. 'And then they did.'

Bibi flings herself at them. I can't move. I'm paralysed with relief and joy.

It doesn't matter.

They come to me.

41

I didn't think I had any tears left inside me, but I do. They pour down my face and get all over Mum and Dad and Bibi and I've never felt anything like it.

We hold each other for so long that the sun's up when we finally stop for breath. When we can finally speak, we go to the tent and talk for ages.

I get the bad news over first.

'This isn't Australia,' I say quietly. 'It's an island in the Pacific Ocean.'

Mum and Dad don't seem that shocked. I get the feeling they already know.

Mum puts her arms round us all. 'We're together,' she says. 'You're safe. That's all I care about.'

She and Dad ask us about our sea journey.

'I'm proud of you, son,' says Dad when I tell him about scooping out the boat.

'Selfish camel-snot,' says Mum when Bibi tells her about the sailor who took the only bucket.

'Exactly,' says Bibi. Then she frowns and looks

around the tent. Some people are talking happily like us, but others are red-eyed and weeping. 'Rashida says,' murmurs Bibi thoughtfully, 'that sometimes people are only camel-snots because of what's happened to them.'

We introduce Mum and Dad to Omar and Rashida.

Mum cries some more when I explain how Rashida's flour saved our lives, and she hugs Rashida for a long time.

'I saved his life too,' says Omar.

Dad hugs him for a long time.

I can see Omar is getting a bit uncomfortable, so I change the subject.

'We've got some good news,' I say to Mum and Dad. 'Bibi's really good at football. She's going to be a football star.'

Bibi glows. She punches me hard on the shoulder. 'So's Jamal,' she says. 'Tell them the plan, Jammy.'

I stare at her.

Jammy?

'A football star needs a nickname,' says Bibi. 'Omar told me.'

I tell Mum and Dad our plan for the future of Afghanistan. About having football careers in Australia and helping form a new government at home so we can all go back safely.

Mum and Dad look at each other and their eyes fill with tears again. I know how they feel. Happiness can do that.

42

Andrew is sitting in a small office in one of the peeling buildings.

'Hello, Jamal,' he says. 'I'm so happy for you.'

I take a deep breath and open my mouth to ask the question I've come to ask.

Before I can, Andrew speaks again. 'I'm also very sorry,' he says. 'I should have told you the truth about this place. I knew you thought it was Australia, but after what you'd been through I couldn't bear to . . .'

He shrugs. I've never seen an Australian look so miserable.

'It's OK,' I say. 'I understand.'

But there's something I don't understand.

'Why did you bring us here?' I ask.

Andrew looks even more miserable.

'The Australian government has changed its refugee policy,' he says. 'That is, they've revised the procedures and protocols. That is. . .'

I watch him struggling to find the right words. I wish he could. The words he's used so far don't sound right for an Australian, not even one speaking my language.

'There was an election in Australia,' he says. 'The Australian government thought they'd get more votes by keeping you out.' His voice goes even quieter and sadder than before. 'And they did.'

I try to understand what Andrew is saying. I think I'm getting the idea. I'm also getting a sick and anxious feeling in my tummy.

Some Australians don't want us.

My head is spinning.

Andrew stands up and goes to a shelf and hands something to me. It's my football.

'I mended it for you,' he says.

I stare at the new patch on top of all the others. It's an Australian flag.

'Thank you,' I say.

I give him a look so he knows I don't just mean about the ball. So he knows I mean about everything.

But I don't understand. Here's a man who's as kind as can be, from a country where people's hearts are bigger than warm loaves, and yet some people there don't want us.

Why?

'Give it a try,' says Andrew, nodding at the ball.

I'm not really in the mood for ball tricks, but Andrew's looking so unhappy I do it to help him feel better. I drop the ball onto my foot and try to flip it to my knee. My hip explodes with pain. I scream and jerk my leg out.

The ball smashes through the window.

'Sorry,' I gasp as I stagger against Andrew's desk.

Andrew doesn't even look at the window. He looks at me, his face creased with worry.

'You poor kid,' he says. 'You need medical attention. And you're not the only one. We haven't even got an X-ray machine.'

He sits down in his chair and puts his head in his hands.

For a second I think it's about the window, but it's not.

'I hate what we're doing to you people,' he says quietly. 'This isn't what I thought we'd be doing and I hate being here and I'm so sorry.'

I can see he's struggling to control his feelings. It's what he's been trained to do. But it's not working, probably because he's been on duty for such long hours lately.

A tear is rolling down his face.

He blinks hard.

I hobble round to his side of the desk and pat him on the arm.

'I'm glad you're here,' I say.

I know how he feels. It can be very sad and lonely, being a long way from home. And having a dream and finding it's going to be harder than you thought.

'Do you know the secret of football?' I ask him.

Andrew shakes his head.

I tell him. 'Never give up,' I say, 'even when things are looking hopeless.'

For some reason this makes Andrew blink even harder, so I put my arm round his shoulders.

He looks up at me with a sad smile.

I smile back and think of all the other Australians there must be who are like Andrew.

'Everything will be OK,' I say to him. 'I know it will.'

I look out of the broken window.

The sea is like a glistening desert in the morning sun.

Down on the beach I can see Mum and Dad and Bibi walking together at the water's edge. Even though they're picking their way through plastic bags and rotting seaweed, they look so happy my chest fills with love and I feel so lucky.

I know this isn't really Australia, but it feels like Australia to me.

Teacher's Notes

For *Boy Overboard* Teacher's Notes, which
include a historical and cultural background to
the events in this story, visit
www.puffin.com.au